Spelling Connections 2

Toni Marasco

Cheryl Lemire

NELSON CANADA

Published in 1987 by
Nelson Canada,
A Division of International Thomson Limited
1120 Birchmount Road
Scarborough, Ontario
M1K 5G4

ISBN 0-17-602281-3

Canadian Cataloguing in Publication Data

Marasco, Toni
Spelling Connections 2

For use in schools.
ISBN 0-17-602281-3

1. Spellers. 2. English language - Orthography and spelling - Problems, exercises, etc. I. Lemire, Cheryl. II. Title.

PE1145.2.M36 1987 428.1 C87-093055-9

Project Manager: Alan Simpson

Contributing Writers: Alan Simpson, Robert Cutting

Editors: Ruta Demery, Terry-Lee Wheelband

Design and Art Direction: Mary Jane Gerber

Cover Design and Illustration: Mary Jane Gerber

Cover Photography: Jeremy Jones

Typesetting: Trigraph Inc.

Printing: The Bryant Press Ltd.

Illustrations:
Heike Blohm: 38, 39 (upper), 96, 117, 119, 121, 130, 136, 144, 145 (lower), 153, 155; David Chang: 37, 39 (lower); Brenda Clark: 15-17; Mark Craig: 81, 82; Susanna Denti: 107-109, 129, 140, 145 (upper); Sharon Foster: 12-14, 31-33, 152; Blake Foy: 110-112; Victor Gad: 50, 52, 78-80, 91-93; Don Gauthier: 24-26, 43, 45, 75, 76, 88-90, 133-135, 141; Mary Jane Gerber: 94, 95; Katherine Helmer: 100-102; Linda Hendry: 22, 23, 60, 61, 128, 138; Nancy Kettles: 113, 114; Vladyana Krykorka: 72-74, 137; Sharon Matthews: 62-64; Glenn Mielke: 18-20, 53, 54, 69-71, 139, 148; Greg Ruhl: 10, 11; David Shaw: 27-30, 46-49, 67, 68, 84-87, 103-106, 123-125, 143, 146, 151; Lisa Smith: 34-36, 97-99; Adriana Taddeo: 131, 142; Lorraine Tuson: 40-42, 56-58; Vlasta Van Kampen: 116, 118; Tracy Walker: handprinting.

Printed and bound in Canada

234567890/BP/65432109

Table of Contents

Print Models

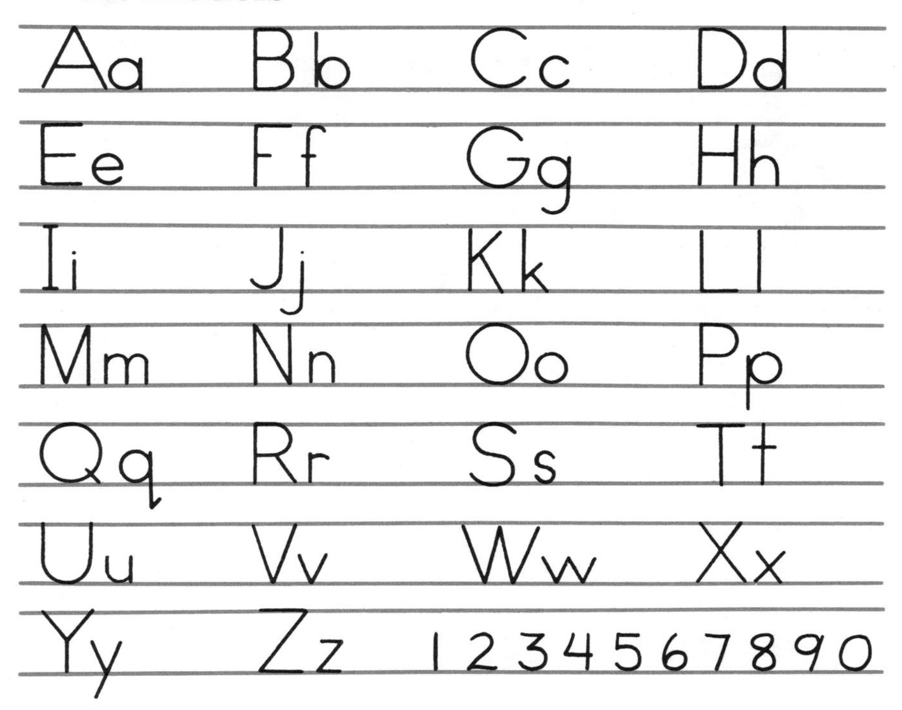

How to Use This Book

15 Winter Changes

an am do back can eat look help what rabbit

Your Class Words

Are there any other words you'd like to add to your list?

Checking What You Know

How many of the words can you already spell?

Meaning Connections

1. **From Brown to White**

(a) Read about how Snowy changes for winter.

Hello. My name is Snowy. I'm a rabbit. I lose my brown summer fur in the fall. My feet, ears, and head turn white first. For a little while I look like ripple ice cream. In ten weeks I'm all white—except my eyes and the tips of my ears. Can you guess what colour they are?

(b) Write a sentence to answer each question.

(1) What colour is Snowy in the summer?

56

(2) When does Snowy begin to turn white?

(3) Why might Snowy change during the winter?

Pattern Connections

1. **Changing**

What word can you make when you add **ing** to **fall**? Some words, like **fall**, just add **ing** = **falling**.

What word do you get when you add **ing** to **make**? Some words, like **make**, drop **e** before adding **ing** = **making**.

(a) Copy the chart below.

Just add **ing**	Drop **e**, then add **ing**
falling	making

(b) Make new words by adding **ing** to each word below. Write the words on your chart.

help like look do bake eat change

(c) Add two more **ing** words to each column.

(d) Pick any three **ing** words. Write a sentence for each word. Like this:

Snowy the rabbit is changing colour.

2. **Rabbits Can**

(a) Many words have the **a** sound in **at** or **and**. Write the List Words and Class Words with this sound.

(b) Use the chart to write other words that have the **a** sound in **at** or **and**. Some of your words may be the names of animals.

At the beginning	In the middle
at	stand

3. **What's That?**

(a) Which List Word has the letters **at** but does **not** rhyme with **meat**?

(b) Write one or two questions about **Winter Changes**. Use that List Word in your questions.

Writing Connections

1. **Changing Reports**

Pick any animal. Tell about that animal by finishing these sentences in your notebook.

Hi! My name is . I look like
I have . I'm a

Checkup

See how many new List Words you can spell this week.

58

List Words/Class Words

Before you begin each Unit, take time to talk about the things you will be reading about. Talk about the **List Words**. Add other words that you would like to learn to spell. These are **Your Class Words**.

Checking What You Know

Here you will find out which List Words and Class Words you can already spell. You will also find out which parts of words are problems for you.

Meaning Connections

Before you can use a word, you need to know what it means. In this section you will choose the best List Words to complete stories and poems. You will find out that some words can have many meanings. You will also discover words that mean almost the same as other words, and words that are opposites.

Pattern Connections

Many words have families—just like people. Here you will discover families of words where some of the sounds are the same but are spelled differently. You will also find words that share the same pattern of letters. Knowing about word families will help you spell the many new words you will meet in school and at home.

Writing Connections

Here you will use the words you have learned. You may write a poem, a story, or sentences.

Checkup

At the end of the Unit you will see how many List Words and Class Words you can now spell. You will also see which words are still giving you problems. Collect these problem words in your **Personal Spelling Dictionary** to help you with your writing.

Backup/Wordworks

Every sixth Unit is a special review called **Backup**. You will be looking back at the List Words and using them in games, riddles, and puzzles.
The **Wordworks** page in each Backup Unit lets you write about interesting things in exciting new ways.

Superconnections

There are some exciting word games and puzzles in the back of this book. Find out more about words and make your writing power grow. Your teacher will show you which activities are just for **you**.

Spelling Is for Writing

Why is it important to spell correctly?

When is it important to spell correctly?

Share your ideas with your classmates.

Help Yourself with These Study Steps

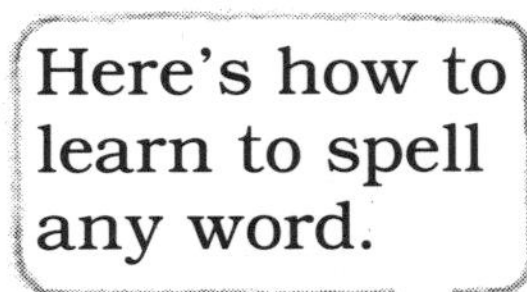

STEP 1, Look and Study

Look at the word. Say it to yourself. See how its sounds are spelled.

STEP 2, Picture

Picture the word in your mind.

STEP 3, Write and Check

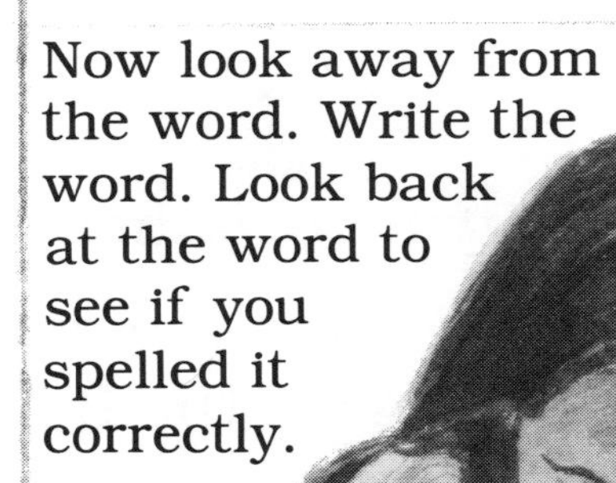

Now look away from the word. Write the word. Look back at the word to see if you spelled it correctly.

If you still need help, go back to Step 1.

1 Good News!

oh said good the fly duck day

Your Class Words

Choose three more words to add to your list.

Checking What You Know

The Study Steps on page 11 will help you to spell any words you missed.

Meaning Connections

1. **Oh, Good!**

   (a) Read this rhyme together.

   "Good show," cried the crow.
   "Good try," buzzed the fly.
   "Good luck," quacked the duck.
   "Good day," sang the jay.
   "Good tune," called the loon.
   "What a good talk," said
   the flock.

   (b) Copy this chart in your notebook.

Things that fly	Words for said
loon	quacked

(c) Write the words from the rhyme that fit in each column.

(d) Add two of your own words to each column.

Pattern Connections

1. **The Duck Pond**

(a) Use the letters inside the duck pond to make words that start with **th**. One is done for you.

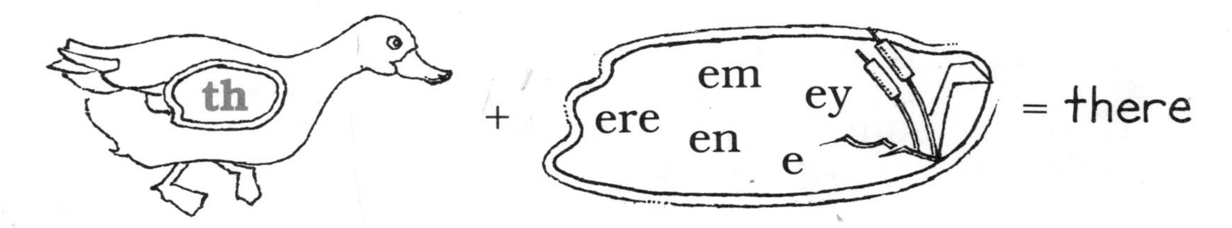

(b) Use three of your **th** words in sentences about ducks. For example:

There are six ducks quacking.

2. **Spelling Tricks**

You can remember how to spell a tricky word by using each of its letters in a silly saying.

(a) Which List Word does this silly saying spell?

silly alligators in dresses

(b) Write a silly saying to help you spell **the**.

3. **Play With Jay**

(a) Write the **ay** List Word in your notebook.

(b) Help Jay find other **ay** words. Use the beginning letters shown and one of your own beginnings. One word is done for you.

(c) Use your **ay** words to complete this rhyme:

My name is Jay.
Would you like to ____?
If you ____,
I'll show you the ____.
Okay?

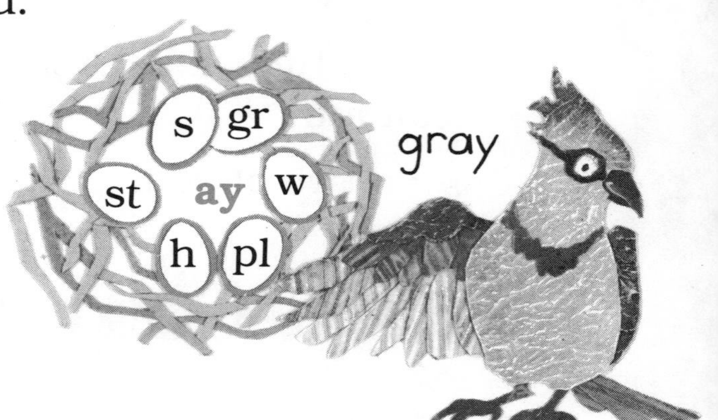

Writing Connections

1. **Good for Me!**

Here are some ways to use the word **good**.

(a) Write at least four other ways you can use the word **good**.

(b) Draw a cartoon of the one you like best.

Checkup

Write in your Personal Spelling Dictionary any words you missed.

2 Leapfrog

fun frog have log sun hop to

Your Class Words

Choose three more words your class would like to spell.

Checking What You Know

Use the Study Steps every day to learn new words.

Meaning Connections

1. **The Frog Race**

   (a) Read this story.

(b) Write the word in the story that
   (1) tells how frogs move.
   (2) tells what kind of time the children had.

(c) Write the List Word that matches each picture.

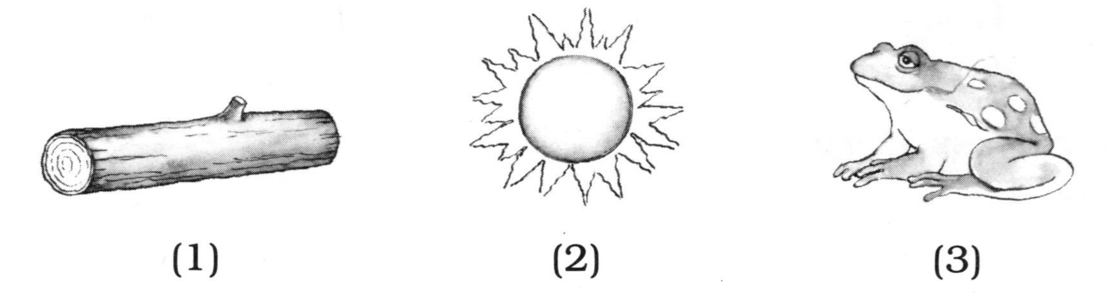

(1) (2) (3)

Pattern Connections

1. **Sun Fun**

(a) Look at the flower. Make rhyming words by adding the letters to **un**. Write the words in your notebook.

(b) Write the word you made that means
   (1) happy times.
   (2) a bright star.
   (3) go fast.
   (4) part of a hot dog.

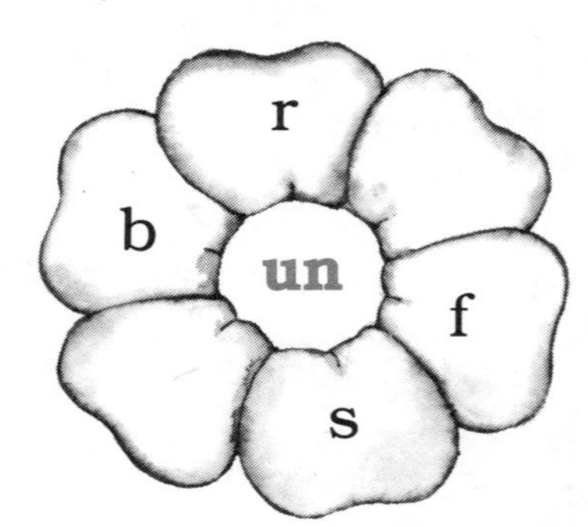

2. **Wordprints**

Copy the shapes below. Write the List Word that belongs in each shape. The first one is done for you.

(a) (b) (c) (d)

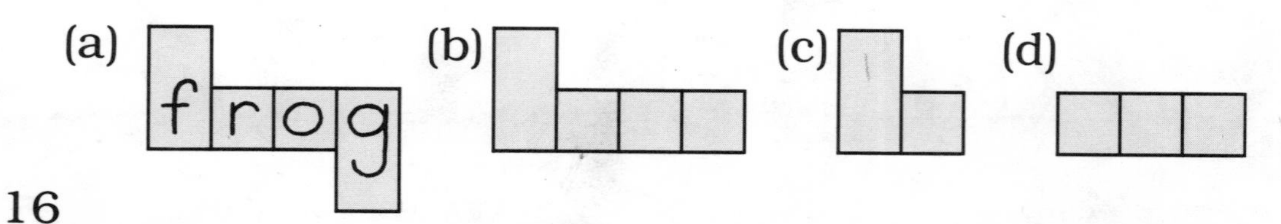

3. **Jog a Log**

(a) Write the List Words that rhyme with **jog**.

(b) Write two other words that rhyme with **jog**.

(c) Write a sentence using two of the words that rhyme with **jog**. Like this:

The dog went for a jog.

Writing Connections

1. **Frog Fun**

Write three sentences about frogs.

▶ Sentences start with capital letters. Does each of your sentences start with a capital letter?

2. **Fun and Games**

Reread the story "The Frog Race." Write a picture story of your own about a game where you hop, leap, or jump. It could be hopscotch, a one-legged race, or leapfrog.

Checkup
How many of your words can you spell now?

3 Three of a Kind

one two little and three pigs bad

Your Class Words

Add three more words to your list.

Checking What You Know

Write the correct spelling of any word you didn't know. Underline the letters you found difficult.

Meaning Connections

1. **Three Little Pigs**

   Write this poem in your notebook.
   Use List Words to complete it.

   Three fat little pigs.
   Two huffs and puffs.
   One big b____ wolf.

   Three scared little p____.
   T____ huffs and puffs.
   One red brick house.

   T____ safe l____ pigs.
   Two huffs a____ puffs.
   O____ thin angry wolf.

2. **How Many?**

Write in your notebook the words that belong with the pictures.

(a) _____ cat

(b) _____ _____

(c) 2

(d) 3

Pattern Connections

1. **It's Dandy!**

(a) Write the **and** words that fit the puzzle. The clues will help you.

(1) I am found on a beach.

(2) I'm at your arm's end, to shake with a friend.

(3) I am fun to eat as a treat.

(4) When music is played, you may hear me.

(1)		a	n	d	
(2)		a	n	d	
(3)		a	n	d	
(4)		a	n	d	

(b) Can you write two other **and** words?

(c) Use two **and** words in a rhyming sentence. Like this:

It's grand to play in the sand.

2. **Wordprints**

(a) Write the List Words that fit in these wordprints.

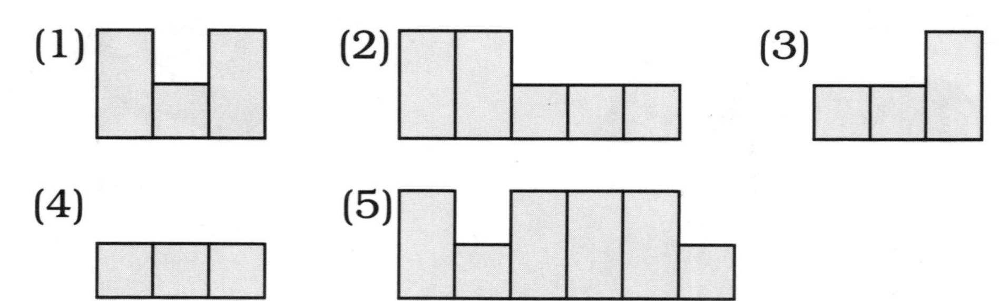

(b) Make a wordprint for one of your Class Words.

Writing Connections

1. **One, Two, Three**

Use each pair of words to write a sentence.

(a) one bad (b) two and (c) three little

2. **Number Rhymes**

Write a number rhyme. Use any three numbers in a row. Use your own ideas or this rhyme pattern:

One, two, three,
Climb a tree.
Three, two, one,
Let's have fun!

Checkup

See how many List Words you can spell now.

4 Fall Again

fall bird into bee day
try cats on tree

Your Class Words

Add words your class would like to spell.

Checking What You Know

Don't forget to use the Study Steps every day.

Meaning Connections

1. **A Fall Report**

Choose the right words that complete the story. Write the words you choose in your notebook.

Who likes to watch weather reports on TV?

"I do," said the [bird / cat / bee], "so I know when to go [into / on / by] my hive."

"I do," said the [bird / cat / bee], "so I know when to fly south."

"I do," said the [tree / bird / bee], "so I know when to make my leaves fall."

Pattern Connections

1. **More Than One**

   To make some words mean more than one you add **s**.

   (a) Complete these sentences with words that mean more than one.

   (1) The buzzed around the .

   (2) The watched the fly away.

   (b) Find three other words that can be made to mean more than one by adding **s**. Write the new words you can make.

2. **Play Day**

   Match the rhyming words. Write them in your notebook.

   bee fall play wall tree day

3. **Try to Catch a Leaf**

   (a) Write the List Word with the **y** sound in **fly**.

   (b) Catch a leaf and make new words that end with **y**.

   (c) Write a question about fall using **why**.

Writing Connections

1. **Fall Changes**

   The long, hot days of summer are over. The days grow shorter. The nights are colder. Fall is here.

   Make a list of changes that happen in the fall.

2. **A Pile of Leaves**

   Look at the picture.

   What is happening in this picture?
   What do you think happened **before**?
   What do you think will happen **next**?
   Write a story about the picture.

Sentences that tell something end with a period. Make sure that each of your telling sentences ends with a period.

Checkup

Add words you had trouble with to your Personal Spelling Dictionary.

5 Country Fair

I me may we have
some ask just red

Your Class Words

Choose three more words to add to your list.

Checking What You Know

Write the correct spelling of any word you didn't know. Use the Pretest chart to show which part of the word was difficult.

Meaning Connections

1. **At the Country Fair**

Use List Words to complete Michael's letter.

Dear Grandmother,

Thank you for taking m____ to the country fair. ____ was glad that Mr. Green's pig won a blue ribbon. S____ of the prize pumpkins were really big. Ms. Lee's pumpkin would

make a great jack-o'-lantern! W_____ are all happy that your pie won a r_____ ribbon.

M_____ I come and visit you again soon?

Love,
Michael

Pattern Connections

1. **Just Crust**

(a) Make new words by adding the letters in the pie to **ust**.

(b) Write one of the new words for each picture clue.

(1) a _____ pan (2) a _____ of bread

(c) Use two **ust** words in a sentence.

2. **Blue Ribbon Pig**

Mr. Green's pig won this. It is not a ribbon. What is it?

Each clue will tell you a letter in the answer.

The first letter is in **pay** but not in **may**.
The second letter is in **red** but not in **bed**.
The third is in **hive** but not in **have**.
The fourth is in **zed** but not in **red**.
The fifth is in **me** but not in **my**.

3. **Milking Contest**

(a) Two words in each pail rhyme. Write the pairs in your notebook.

(b) Add one more rhyming word to each pair.

Writing Connections

1. **What's in a Name?**

Write the name of a place you enjoyed visiting. Write it down instead of across. Use each letter to start a word that tells about the place. Like this:

2. **Friendly Letter**

You have made a new friend at a country fair. Write a letter to her or him. Tell about something exciting that has happened where you live.

The name of a person begins with a capital letter. Did you use capital letters correctly?

Checkup

How many List Words can you spell now?

Backup

and	fall	cats	we	into
oh	fly	said	the	day
bad	pigs	some	tree	fun
good	bee	log	just	hop
little	duck	three	sun	frog
try	bird	I	on	to
red	two	me	have	may
ask				one

1. **Falling Leaves**

How many words can you write using the letters on the falling leaves? You may use a letter more than once.

2. **Picturing Words**

(a) Copy the boxes in your notebook. Write the first letter of each picture word in a box to make a List Word.

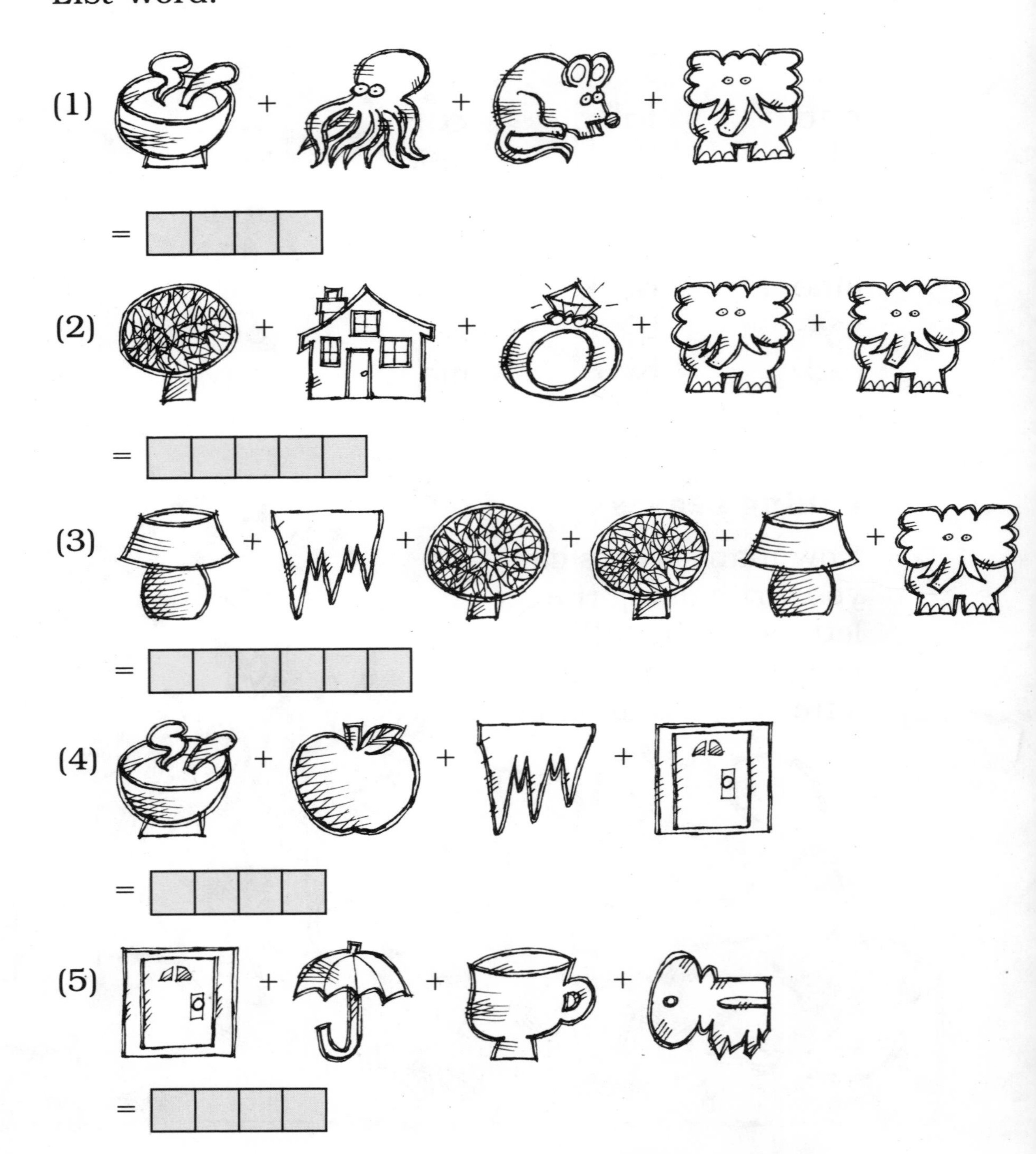

(b) Make three of your own picture words to trade with a friend. Use your List Words.

3. **Word Search**

Look across each row.
Find a List Word.
Write it in your notebook.
The first word is **try**.

c n t r y i
j a n d g t
p l e r e d
g o o d p k
r j u s t l
d e m a y r

4. **Two in a Row**

Some of your List Words have two-letter words in them. Find six of these List Words and write them. Circle the two letters that make a word. Like this:

j(u)(s)t = us

5. **Secret Message**

Use the code to find out Goldilocks's secret message. Write her message in your notebook.

Code: a = ● e = ▲ i = ■ o = ▼ u = ◆

"▼h, g▼▼d!" s●■d
Goldilocks. "This l■ttl▲
bowl ●nd this l■ttl▲
chair look j◆st right for
m▲. ■ think I'll h●v▲
s▼m▲ porridge
t▼ eat."

Wordworks

1. **What's It All About?**

Read these sentences Jay wrote about the sun.

The sun is warm and bright.
It makes me smile.
It helps plants and trees grow.
Sunny days are good days because
I can play outside.

Write sentences to tell about **one** of these:

- frogs
- birds
- pigs
- trees

2. **Small Talk**

Bee is very sad because she cannot find her way home. What does Fly say to make Bee feel better? Draw the cartoon boxes. Write what Fly and Bee say to each other.

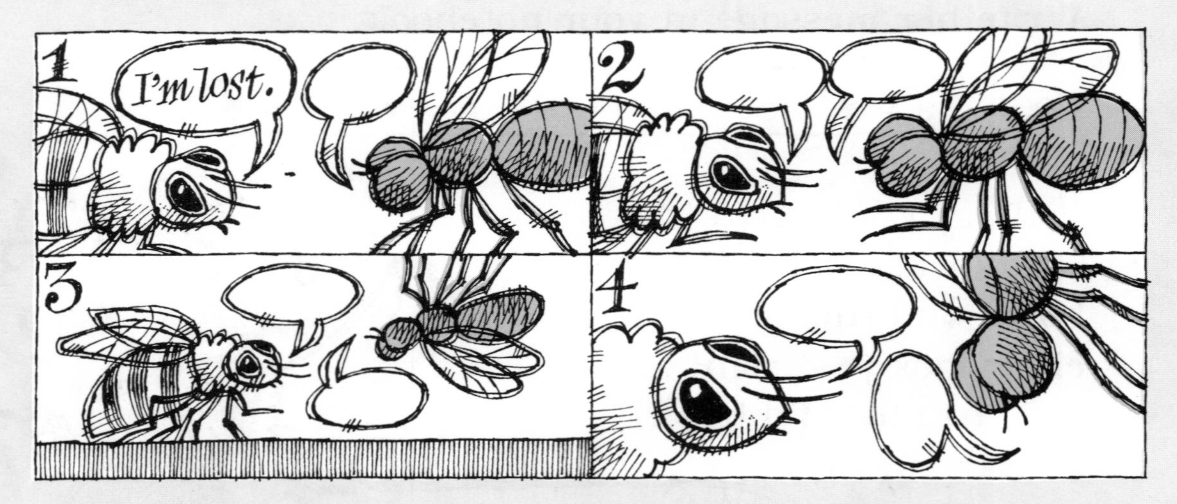

Did you write what you wanted to say? Read your sentences. See if you want to make any changes.

7 Making Masks

mask	out	she	draw	us
cut	then	did	is	ask

Your Class Words

Choose two more words to add to your list.

Checking What You Know

Use the Study Steps on page 11.

Meaning Connections

1. **Making a Mask**

(a) Here are the steps Chad used to make a mask.

1. **Trace** a face on white paper.
2. Paint the eyes and the lips.
3. Cut **around** the face. **Next** cut out holes for the eyes, nose, and mouth.

continued on the next page...

4. Glue big ears and curly hair on the **face**.

5. **Poke** a hole on each side of the mask. Tie strings through the holes.

6. Put on the mask. **Get** someone to tie the strings behind your head.

(b) Write the List Words you could use instead of the words printed **like this**.

Pattern Connections

1. **Special Letters**

Look at this alphabet.

a b c d **e** f g h **i** j k l m n **o** p q r s t **u** v w x y z

The letters printed **like this** are called **vowels**. The other letters are called **consonants**.

Someone spilled paint on the vowels in the List Words. Find the missing vowels and write the words.

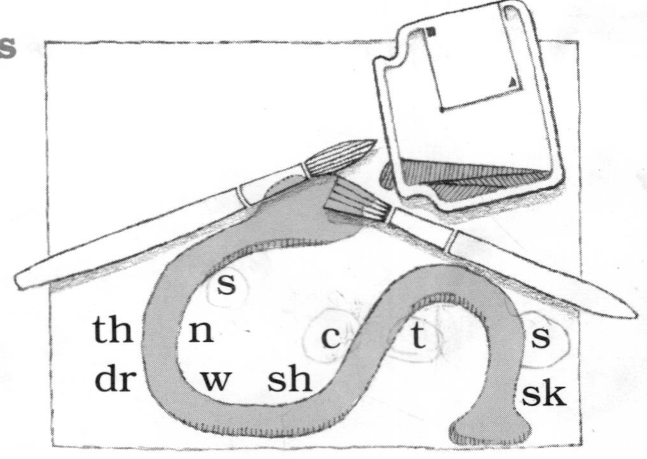

2. **Will It Fit?**

   (a) Write the two List Words that have the **i** sound in **it**.

   (b) Find three words in the steps for making a mask that have the **i** sound in **it**.

   (c) Write a sentence about making a mask. Use as many of your **i** words as you can.

Writing Connections

1. **Telling How**

   Remember the steps Chad used to make his mask? Write the steps for making this paper bag mask.

1. 

2. 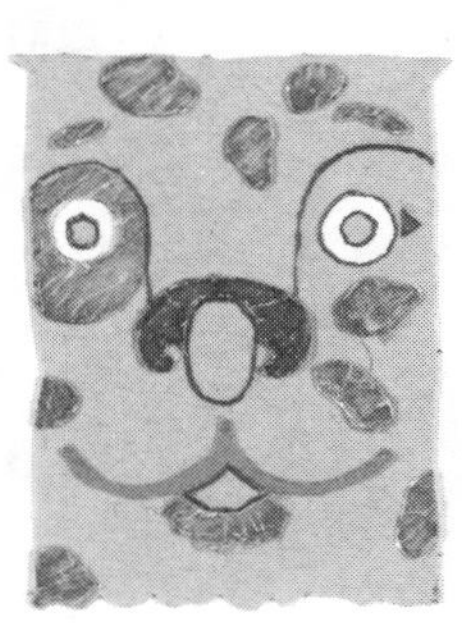

3. 

4. 

Checkup

Write in your Personal Spelling Dictionary any words you missed.

Costume Party Time

bunny
silly
funny
old
brother
his
her
mother
brown

Your Class Words

Add three more words to your list.

Checking What You Know

How many of your words can you already spell?

Meaning Connections

1. **Chad's Clown Suit**

Finish this story. Write the missing List Words in your notebook.

Chad was going to a costume party. His clown mask was ready. Now Chad needed a f___ clown suit.
H___ mother gave him a pair of o___ baggy pants. She found some s___ looking socks with purple dots. She also gave Chad h___ shirt with big red flowers on it.
Chad looked at his clown suit. Something was missing. Chad knew just what it was...

Pattern Connections

1. **Witch's Brew**

   (a) Write the List Words that have the same beginning sound as **br**ing.

   (b) Fill in the blanks and write the words.

   (1) (2) (3)

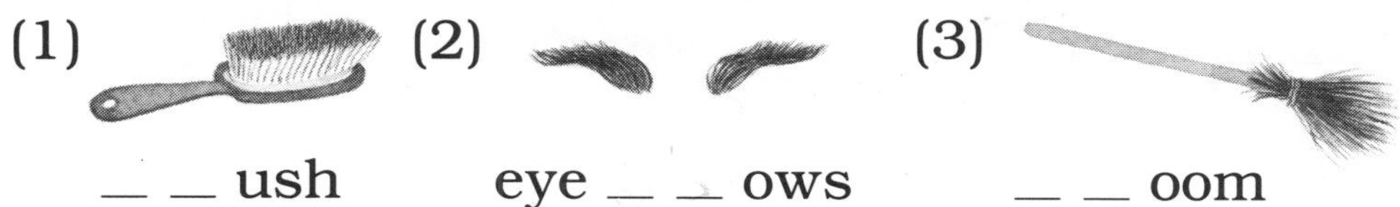

   _ _ ush   eye _ _ ows   _ _ oom

   (c) Complete this story using **br** words.

   Chad's sister dressed as a witch. She painted big, black ____ on her face. She carried a long ____. She had a ____ coloured pot. In the pot was a witch's **br**ew.

2. **Double Trouble**

   (a) Ghosts have covered up some letters in three List Words. Write the words.

   si__y   fu__y   bu__y

   (b) Find four more words with **ll** and **nn** in them.

3. **Another Surprise**

   (a) Two people in Chad's family are hiding inside these costumes. Unscramble the words to find out who they are.

   (b) Use each word in a sentence about a costume.

Writing Connections

1. **Exploding Sentences**

   Here is a way to "explode" a sentence to add **describing words.**

   Chad made a [scary / silly / clown] mask.

   This sentence is found in the "exploded" one:

   Chad made a clown mask.

   Add your own words to explode the following sentence. Write three different sentences.

   Chad's sister wore a [______ / ______ / ______] costume.

2. **What's Missing?**

   Read the story "Chad's Clown Suit" again. What do you think Chad was missing? Write your own ending to the story.

   Read your ending. Can you add describing words to make it more interesting?

Checkup

How many of your words can you spell now?

9 My Pet and I

my
puppy
so
ball
get
all
pet
but
not
little

Your Class Words

Are there any other words you'd like to add to your list?

Checking What You Know

Use the Study Steps every day to learn new words.

Meaning Connections

1. **My Puppy and I**

   (a) Read the poem to find out how Jill and her pet are alike. How are they different?

   My puppy has brown eyes and so do I.
   My puppy drinks milk and so do I.
   My puppy chews slippers. . .but I don't!

   My puppy likes running and so do I.
   My puppy gets dirty and so do I.
   My puppy hates baths. . .but I don't!

(b) Copy this chart. List the things the puppy and Jill both do. List the things only the puppy does.

How they are alike	How they are different
My puppy and I...	My puppy...
drink milk	

(c) Write other things you think the puppy and Jill both do. Add one thing only the puppy does.

Pattern Connections

1. **Let's Play Ball**

(a) Find six words that rhyme with **tall**. Use the beginning letters on the ball. Use one of your own beginnings.

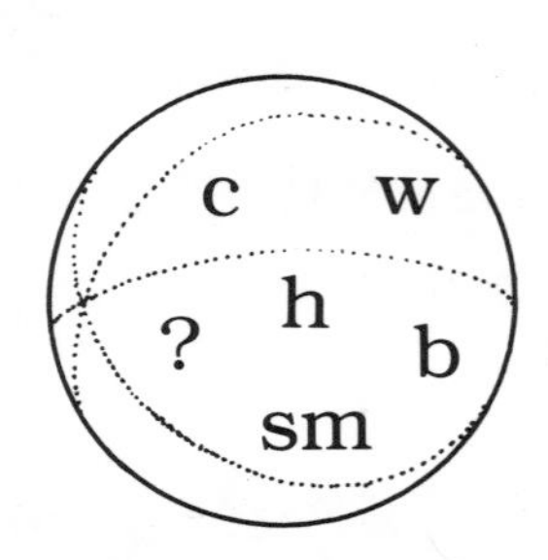

(b) Use two of your **all** words to write rhyming verses. Like this:

My puppy chases the ball,
As I roll it down the hall.

2. **A Wet Pet**

Copy and complete these sentences. The missing words all rhyme with **pet**.

(a) Cats do not like to get _____.

(b) Butterflies are caught with a _____.

(c) If you find a snake, _____ it go.

(d) A vet is a doctor who helps a sick _____.

3. **That Cat!**

Some little words are hiding in bigger words.
Like this: at c**at**

Write the List Words that have these words in them.

(a) up (b) all (c) it (d) no

Writing Connections

1. **Pet Words**

Write a sentence with each pair of words.

(a) puppy but (b) get so (c) little not

2. **The Pet for Me**

Choose an animal you would like to have as a pet.
Here are some you could choose.

fish kitten bird monkey

Write sentences or verses to tell
how you and your pet are
alike and different.

Checkup

See how many List Words you can spell now.

10 C.T.'s Toy Store

off
store
doll
game
new
toy
with
joy
like
fun

Your Class Words

Add words your class would like to spell.

> **Checking What You Know**
>
> Write the correct spelling of any word you didn't know. Use the Pretest chart to show which part of the word was difficult.

Meaning Connections

1. **A Birthday Gift to Share**

   Here is a story Marco wrote in his journal. Write the List Words that complete the story.

   Today was my mom's day o____. We went to C.T.'s toy s____. I wanted to buy my sister Lisa a d____ for her birthday. We found one w____ big brown eyes. It looked just l____ Lisa.

   My mom thought I should buy a g____ instead. Mom was right! Lisa and I both had f____ playing the n____ game.

2. **The Word Store**

   Shop for words. Write the List Word that

   (a) is the opposite of **old**.

   (b) means the same as a **shop**.

   (c) is the opposite of **on**.

   (d) tells how you feel about a friend.

Pattern Connections

1. **Crossword Fun**

   Copy the shapes below. Add letters to make crossword pairs that rhyme. Your List Words will help you.

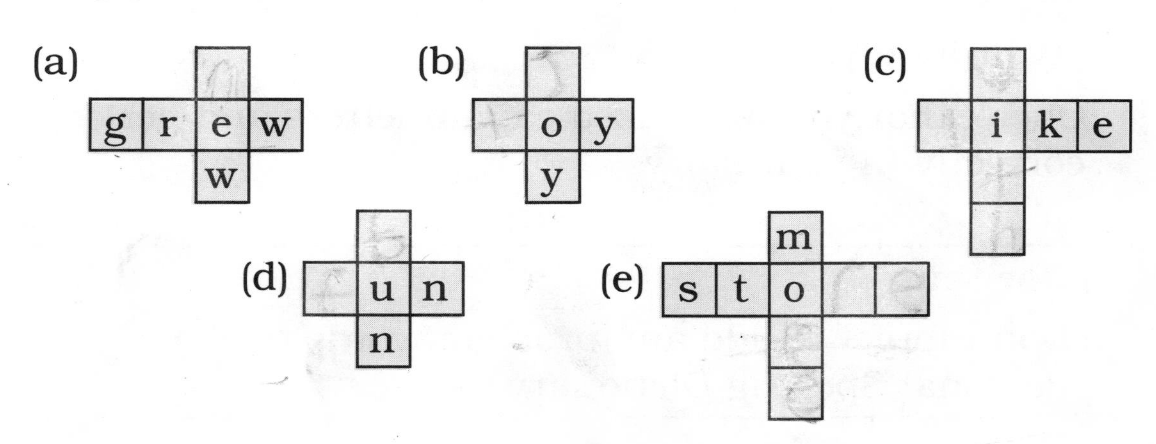

2. **Name Game**

(a) Follow the arrows to play this game. Move the **ame** game piece to each box to make a new word. Write the words in your notebook. For the last two boxes, write your own **ame** words.

(b) Use two or more of your **ame** words in a sentence about playing a game.

Writing Connections

1. **Play Along**

Complete this sentence in your notebook.

I like to play _____ because _____.

2. **My Favourite Toy**

Do you have a toy that is very special to you? What is it? When did you get it? Why do you like it?

Write a journal story about the day you got your favourite toy.

▶ Check that you have used capital letters and periods correctly in your story.

Checkup

Don't forget to add any problem words to your Personal Spelling Dictionary.

11 Ah-choo!

blue got cold sick hot
down feet up at me

Your Class Words

Choose three more words to add to your list.

Checking What You Know

See how many of the words you already know.

Meaning Connections

1. **Sniffles**

   (a) Read this poem.

   My head is hot.
   My feet are cold.
   Br--rr--**RR**!

   My eyes are wet.
   My throat is dry.
   Cough, cough, **COUGH**!

   I'm all stuffed up.
   I'm feeling down.
   Ah--ah--**CHOO**!

   I think I've got a c--c--**cold**!

(b) The words **happy** and **sad** are opposites. Write each word with its opposite. Use words from the poem "Sniffles."

dry   down   hot   head

Pattern Connections

1. **Wordprints**

(a) Write the List Words that fit in these wordprints.

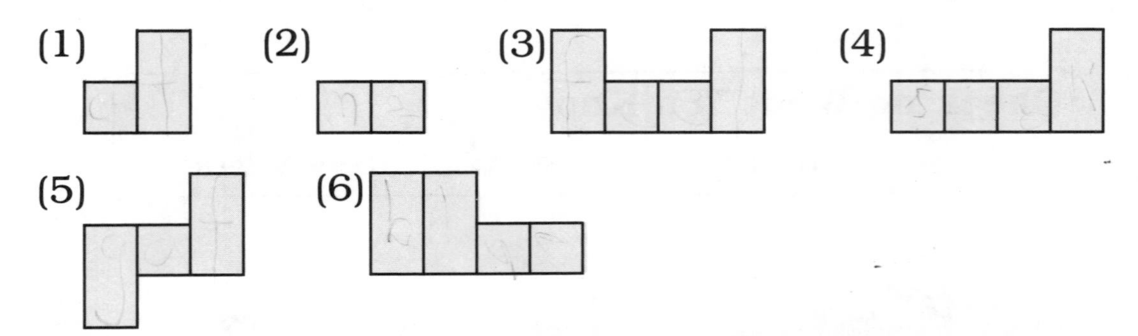

(b) Make a wordprint for one of your Class Words.

2. **Feeling Cold**

(a) Write the **old** words to complete the puzzle.

(1) not hot
(2) bright yellow
(3) took money for something
(4) said something
(5) keeping something in your hands
(6) bending paper or cloth

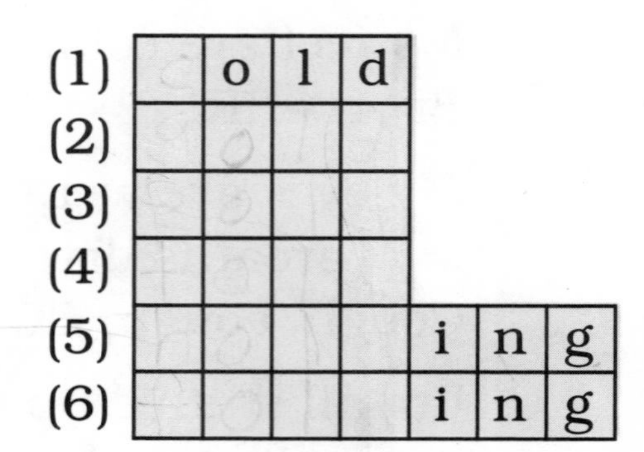

(b) Use two **old** words in a sentence.

3. **C--C--Cold**

Use the picture clues to write words that begin with the **c** sound in **cold**.

(a) _ _ _

(d) _ _ _

(b) _ _ _

(e) _ _ _ _

(c) _ _ _

(f) _ _ _ _ _

Writing Connections

1. **More Sniffles**

Read the poem "Sniffles" again. Use the pattern below to write your own poem.

My _____ is/are _____.
I'm feeling _____.
_____ _____ _____!
(sounds)

▶ Give your poem a title.

Checkup
See how many List Words you can spell now.

Backup

blue	but	doll	then	she
so	bunny	cold	store	puppy
at	not	hot	is	pet
up	ask	feet	her	new
down	little	my	his	silly
draw	fun	mother	got	us
all	me	mask	joy	sick
ball	brown	funny	toy	like
cut	brother	get	old	with
out	did	game	off	

1. **Wordmaker**

   Use the letters **a** and **o** with any of the other letters to make words. You may use each letter more than once. Write as many words as you can.

a

t b l d r w

n g m h

o

GLUE

2. Masked Patterns

Use the beginning letters below and the masked patterns to make words. Write the words in your notebook. One is done for you.

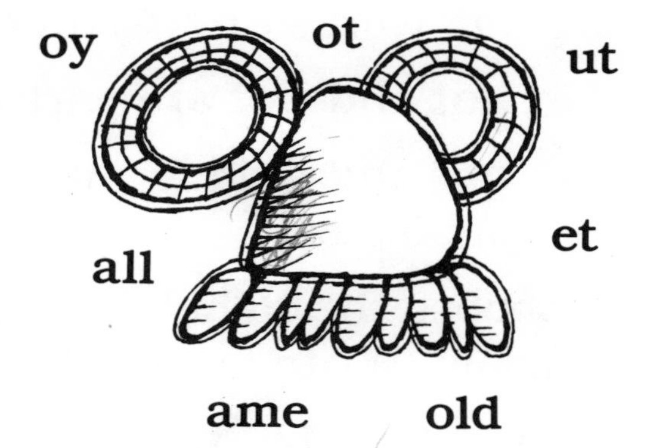

Do it like this:

(a) n = nut, net, name

(b) s = sold, ____, ____

(c) g = ____, ____, ____, ____

(d) b = ____, ____, ____, ____

(e) h = ____, ____, ____

(f) c = ____, ____, ____, ____

(g) j = ____, ____, ____

(h) f = ____, ____, ____

3. Hidden Words

Find the small words hiding in each of these words.
Do it like this:

about—a, out

(a) bunny (c) then (e) mask (g) off (i) ball

(b) toy (d) store (f) mother (h) some

4. **Partner Words**

Some words are partners because they go together:

- **hot** and **not** are partners because they rhyme
- **hot** and **cold** are partners because they are opposites

Choose the right List Word partner for each word below. Write both of the partner words.

(a) wet (b) funny (c) name (d) tall

(e) up (f) didn't (g) him (h) you

5. **Where Is the Puppy Going?**

Use the words **in**, **out**, **up**, or **down** to tell where the puppy is going. Like this:

The puppy is going up the stairs.

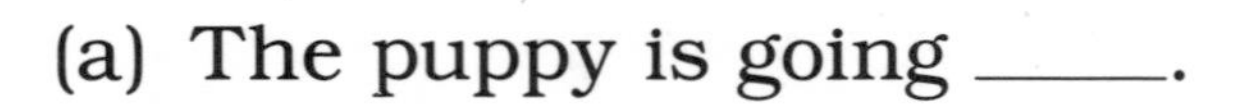

(a) The puppy is going ____.

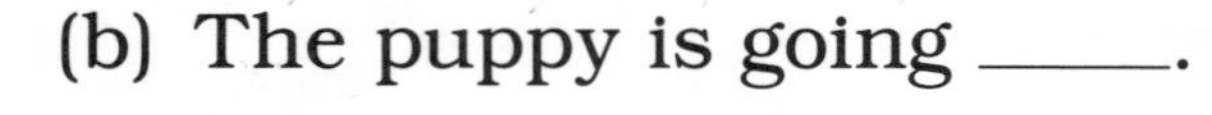

(b) The puppy is going ____.

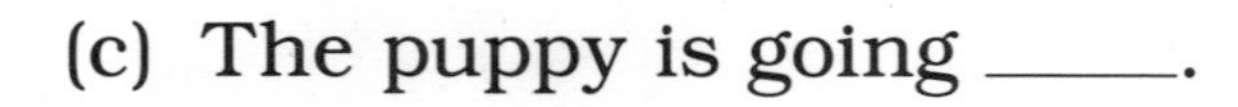

(c) The puppy is going ____.

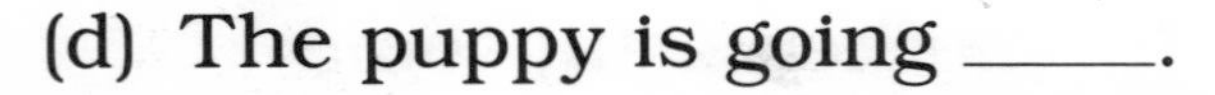

(d) The puppy is going ____.

Wordworks

1. **Sentence Circles**

   Write as many sentences or questions as you can using the words in the circles.

   (a) not and toys games fun silly are puppy

   (b) my up down out brother off puppy got

   Like this: Are games and toys fun? My puppy got up.

2. **What Happened?**

   Harjit likes to go to the zoo. Karen likes to visit the toy store.

   (a) Name three places **you** like to go.

   (b) Choose **one** of your favourite places. Write a story to tell about something that happened or **could** happen there.

▶ Trade your story with a partner. Can you think of ways to make each other's story more exciting?

13 Bear Hugs

hug
are
run
bear
him
about
feel
make
they
just

Your Class Words

Choose three more words to add to your list.

Checking What You Know

Write any words you spelled incorrectly. Underline the letters you found difficult.

Meaning Connections

1. **I Love Hugs**

Finish the story. Write the missing List Words in your notebook.

Hugs are wonderful. Hugs m____ me smile. T____ make me f____ loved. When I'm hugged, I know someone cares a____ me. Just one big h____ makes me happy all day. Hugs a____ such fun.

Pattern Connections

1. **What Goes With <u>ake</u>?**

Write the **ake** word that completes each group of words.

(a) birthday □**ake**

(b) boat on a □**ake**

(c) chocolate milk □□**ake**

(d) snow □□**ake**

(e) □**ake**-believe

2. **Changing Hugs**

(a) Change the beginning letters. Write the new rhyming words.

(1) run → □un → □un → □un

(2) must → □ust → □ust → □□ust

(3) bug → □ug → □ug → □ug

(b) Change the ending letters. Write the new words.

(1) his → hi□ → hi□ → hi□

(2) bug → bu□ → bu□ → bu□

(3) rug → ru□ → ru□ → ru□□

3. **What Are Hugs?**

Using two List Words, write the missing letters in your notebook. Then use your own ideas to finish each sentence.

(a) Hugs ar_ wonderful.

(b) The_ a_ _ ____.

(c) _he_ _re ____.

(d) _ _ _ _ _ _ _ ____.

Writing Connections

1. **Time for Hugs**

Finish each sentence. Tell why hugs are fun.

(a) I like to hug because ____.

(b) Hugs are ____ because ____.

2. **Hug Buttons**

Draw three hug buttons. Write a new sentence about hugs on each button.

Checkup

How many of your words can you spell now?

14 Goldilocks

Mr.	went	of	dear
Mrs.	you	in	
Ms.	for	when	

Your Class Words

Add two or three more words to your list.

Checking What You Know

Don't forget the Study Steps. See page 11.

Meaning Connections

1. **Dear Bears**

   Finish the letter from Goldilocks. Write the missing List Words in your notebook.

   D___ Mr. and M___ Bear,

   Yesterday I was looking f___ someone to play with. I came to your house. W___ I knocked on your door, no one answered. So I w___ i___.

   Thank y___ for the bowl o___ porridge. It was so good.

   Your friend,
   Goldilocks

Pattern Connections

1. **Mrs., Ms., Miss, and Mr.**

   (a) Finish these sentences. Choose List Words.

   (1) ____ means a married woman.

   (2) **Miss** means an unmarried woman.

   (3) ____ is a combination of **Mrs**. and **Miss**.

   (4) ____ means "Mister" or any man.

   (b) Use **Mr.**, **Mrs.**, **Ms.**, or **Miss** and write:

   - your father's, grandfather's, or uncle's last name
   - your mother's, grandmother's, or aunt's last name
   - the last name of a girl in your class
   - your teacher's name

2. **M 4 U (I Am for You)**

   Use the secret code. Write what Baby Bear said to Goldilocks.

   (a) C U 8 all m porridge.

   (b) Y did U break m chair?

   (c) C m chair was 2 little 4 U.

   (d) want 2 know if U R coming 2 C me.

3. **The Letters en**

(a) Copy this chart. Write two or three words under each heading. Use List Words and other words you know.

_en	_end	_ent

(b) Write one or two sentences that ask questions. Use words from your chart.

Writing Connections

1. **The Bear Facts**

Write four questions you would like to ask Goldilocks **or** the Three Bears. Use the code for some of the words.

Sentences that ask something end with a question mark. Does each of your questions end with a question mark?

Word	Code
one, won	1
to, too, two	2
for, four	4
I	
see, sea	C
be, bee	B
ate	8
you	U
are	R
why	Y

2. **Dear Goldilocks**

Pretend you are one of the Three Bears. Write a letter back to Goldilocks.

Checkup

Add any problem words to your Personal Spelling Dictionary.

15 Winter Changes

an can help
am eat what
do look rabbit
back

Your Class Words

Are there any other words you'd like to add to your list?

Checking What You Know

How many of the words can you already spell?

Meaning Connections

1. **From Brown to White**

(a) Read about how Snowy changes for winter.

Hello. My name is Snowy. I'm a rabbit. I lose my brown summer fur in the fall. My feet, ears, and head turn white first. For a little while I look like ripple ice cream. In ten weeks I'm all white—except my eyes and the tips of my ears. Can you guess what colour they are?

(b) Write a sentence to answer each question.

(1) What colour is Snowy in the summer?

(2) When does Snowy begin to turn white?

(3) Why might Snowy change during the winter?

Pattern Connections

1. **Changing**

What word can you make when you add **ing** to **fall**? Some words, like **fall**, just add **ing** = **falling**.

What word do you get when you add **ing** to **make**? Some words, like **make**, drop **e** before adding **ing** = **making**.

(a) Copy the chart below.

Just add **ing**	Drop **e**, then add **ing**
falling	making

(b) Make new words by adding **ing** to each word below. Write the words on your chart.

help like look do bake eat change

(c) Add two more **ing** words to each column.

(d) Pick any three **ing** words. Write a sentence for each word. Like this:

Snowy the rabbit is changing colour.

2. **Rabbits Can**

(a) Many words have the **a** sound in **at** or **and**. Write the List Words and Class Words with this sound.

(b) Use the chart to write other words that have the **a** sound in **at** or **and**. Some of your words may be the names of animals.

At the beginning	In the middle
at	stand

3. **What's That?**

(a) Which List Word has the letters **at** but does **not** rhyme with **meat**?

(b) Write one or two questions about **Winter Changes**. Use that List Word in your questions.

Writing Connections

1. **Changing Reports**

Pick any animal. Tell about that animal by finishing these sentences in your notebook.

Hi! My name is ____.
I have ____.
I look like ____.
I'm a ____.

Checkup

See how many new List Words you can spell this week.

16 Lost and Found

put that mitten yes very
Mom find kitten lost said

Your Class Words

Choose three more words. Add them to your list.

Checking What You Know

Write the correct spelling of any word you didn't know.

Meaning Connections

1. **The Lost Mitten**

Write the List Words that finish this story.

Jess looked out the window and saw t_____ the yard was covered in snow. "Oh, boy!" he s_____.

Jess asked his mother if he could go outside to play. "Y_____, you may," his mother said.

Jess p_____ on his coat, his winter boots, and his hat.

But when he went to put on his m_____s, he could only find one. Jess looked everywhere, but he could not f_____ the other one.

"M_____," asked Jess, "have you seen my mitten?"

Jess's mother laughed. "No, but you have a very lumpy head," she said.

Where was Jess's l_____ mitten?

Pattern Connections

1. **Stay Put**

   Write the **thing** that goes with each **action**. One is done for you.

	Actions	**Things**
(a)	put on coats	puzzles
(b)	put away ____	candles
(c)	put out ____	pencils
(d)	put down ____	coats
(e)	put together ____	toys

2. **Lost Letters**

   (a) Find the lost letters that finish each word. Write the words in your notebook.

   mi☐☐en   si☐☐y
   ki☐☐en   Da☐☐y
   li☐☐le   pu☐☐y
   ra☐☐it   Mo☐☐y

   (b) Write two of your own lost-letter words.

3. **Finding a Pair**

   (a) Write word pairs using the word **very**. Do it like this:
   very cold

   (b) Write a sentence with each word pair you made. Like this:
   The winter wind is very cold.

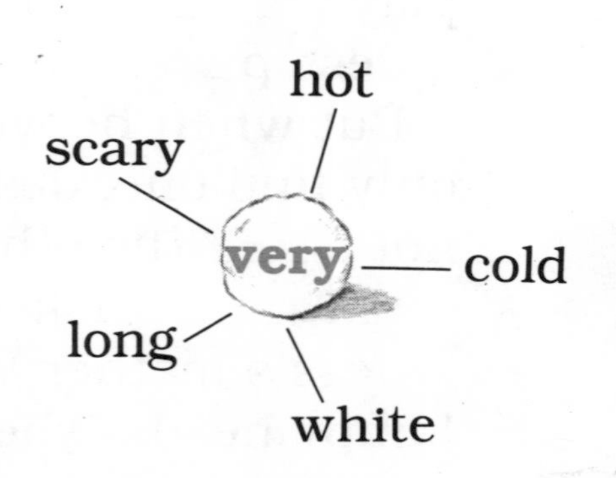

Writing Connections

1. **Happy Endings**

   Write three sentences that tell what happened **next** in the story, "The Lost Mitten." You might want to use these sentence starters:

   - Jess felt _____
   - He _____ and _____
   - There was _____

2. **Finders Keepers**

   Have you or a friend ever lost something? Write a story to tell what was lost. Tell how it was found.

   Trade your story with a friend. Check each other's spelling and use of periods and question marks.

Checkup

See how many List Words you can spell now.

17 No Place Like Home

no
go
or
use

nest
owl
home

where
horse
when

Your Class Words

Add words your class would like to spell.

Checking What You Know

Use the Study Steps to learn new words.

Meaning Connections

1. **Winter Homes**

   Read or listen to the poem. Try to answer the questions about animals in winter.

   Where do cows or horses stay
   When the grass is covered with snow?
   When winter turns the pond to ice,
   Where do the little bullfrogs go?

   Where does the hoot owl make its nest?
   Where does the rabbit hide?
   Where does the bear sleep safe and warm
   When the weather is cold outside?

2. **I Wonder Where?**

Write a question beginning with **what**, **where**, or **when** for each answer. Do it like this:

Rabbits hide in their holes. Where do rabbits hide in winter?

(a) Horses or cows stay in barns.

(b) Owls build nests in tall trees.

(c) The bear's home is a cave.

Pattern Connections

1. **Winter Is Best**

Make new words by adding the beginning letters in the nest to **est**.

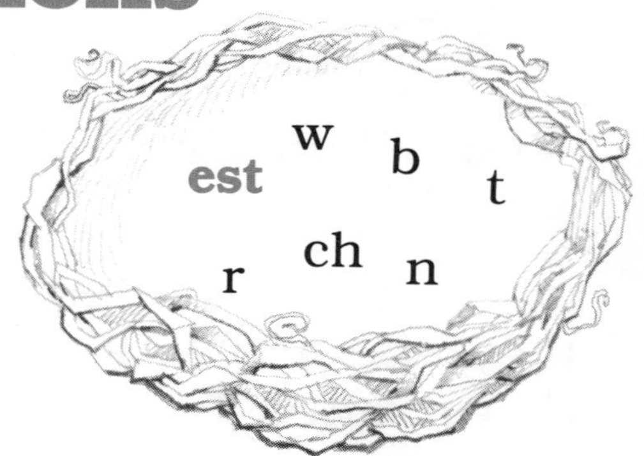

2. **Oh, What a Rhyme!**

Finish these sentences in your notebook. Use words that rhyme with **oh**.

(a) Where do animals ____ in the winter?

(b) It was ____ cold that the horses stayed in the barn.

(c) There is ____ room in the cave for the bears.

(d) When Santa laughs, he says ____ ____ ____.

3. **Time for ing**

(a) Add **ing** to each word printed **like this**. Complete the sentences in your notebook.

use (1) The owl is ____ our tree for a home.

go (2) She is ____ to stay all winter.

hide (3) The bear is ____ in his cave.

sleep (4) He will be ____ all winter.

(b) Make up sentences of your own about animals. Use at least two **ing** words.

Writing Connections

1. **Home Sweet Home**

Write as many words as you can think of that belong with **homes**.

homes

2. **Who, What, Where, Why, When?**

If animals could talk, what kinds of questions about winter might they ask? Write questions they might ask. Use the question words: **who**, **what**, **where**, **why**, **when**.

Checkup

Which words should you add to your Personal Spelling Dictionary?

Backup

hug	what	rabbit	no	owl
an	went	mitten	go	can
am	him	kitten	you	eat
just	they	feel	very	or
yes	lost	do	that	in
home	find	make	dear	back
are	about	look	use	Mom
when	Ms.	of	bear	help
where	Mr.	said	for	horse
run	Mrs.	put	nest	

1. **Crossword Action**

Copy this crossword puzzle. Print List Words to finish it. The arrows show you which way to print the answer to each clue.

Actions

1 ↓ to do or build

2 → she **is**, I ____

3 → to touch

3 ↓ opposite of **lose**

4 ↓ to love

5 ↓ to place

6 → has gone, rhymes with **tent**

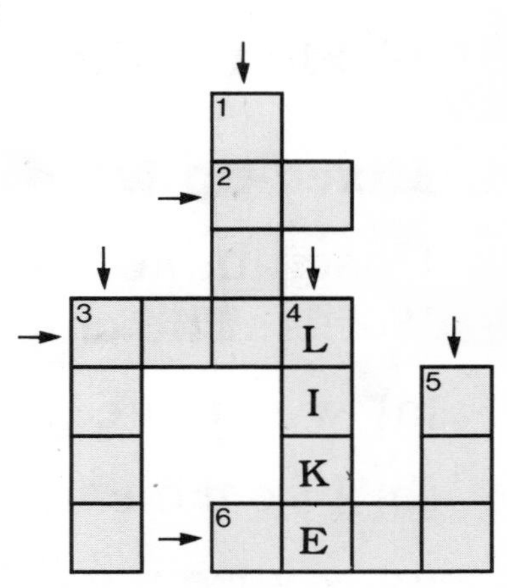

2. **Letter Squares**

(a) Use the letters in squares to make five List Words. Write the words in your notebook. Do it like this:

w	h	r
a	e	e
s	t	n

- The letters in a word must be in squares that touch each other.
- Each letter square can be used only once in a word. For example:

w	h	r
a	e	**e**
s	**t**	n

ate

(b) How many other words can you make?

3. **Partner Words**

(a) Some words can be partners, like **came** and **went**. Use the List Words to find a partner for these words.

(1) ____ and Dad
(2) y____ and me
(3) ____ and out
(4) l____ and found
(5) b____ and front
(6) her and ____
(7) this and th____
(8) c____ and can't

(b) Find other sets of partners in your List Words.

4. **Mixed-up Words**

Unscramble each group of letters to make **two** List Words. The clues will help you.

(a) w w e h e n r t e (2 **w** words)

(b) l f o e o e k l (actions your hands and eyes do)

(c) y y r e v s e (each word has a **y**)

(d) m g h o o e (what you do when you leave school)

5. **Word Race**

Reach the Winner's Circle! Write all of the List Words that belong in each part of the racetrack.

Winner's Circle

First place = 40-46 words

Second place = 30-39 words

Third place = 20-38 words

Fourth place = 1-20 words

Wordworks

1. Alphabet Bits

Use part of the alphabet. Write a list of **homes** or **people** that begin with those letters. For example:

People

A is for [aunts.
astronauts.

B is for ____.

C is for ____.

Homes

A is for ____.

B is for ____.

C is for [cave.
cabin.

2. Animal Alphabet Actions

Write an animal alphabet rhyme. Use the letters A, B, C, and D. You may use your own ideas or this writing pattern.

Apes, apes, apes [eating purple grapes.
or
listening to their tapes.

Bears, bears, bears ____________.

C. . .

D . . .

▶ Who else might enjoy reading your rhyme?

19 What Goes "Pop"?

box book orange gum ring use
pop your by gun snap

Your Class Words

Choose two or three more words. Add them to your list.

Checking What You Know

Write the correct spelling of any word you didn't know.

Meaning Connections

1. **Pop Word Rings**

   Write the List Words that finish the word rings.

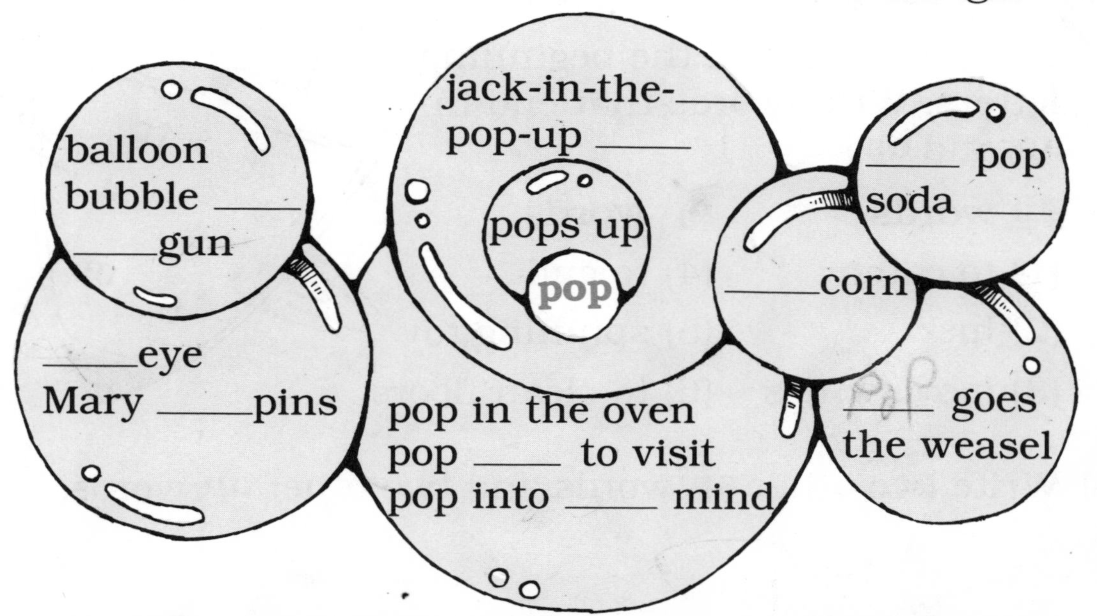

2. **Pop By**

Write a sentence with each of these:

(a) pop-up storybook (c) pops into your mind

(b) jack-in-the-box (d) popped

Pattern Connections

1. **R-r-r-ing!**

Finish the sentences. Write **ing** words using the letters on the ring.

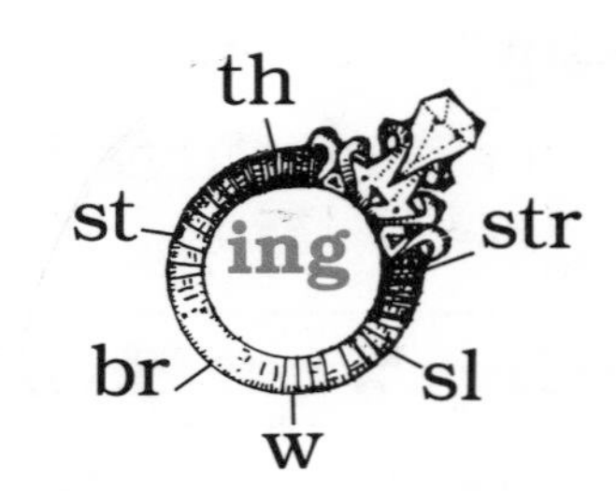

(a) We tied a _____ to the kite.

(b) Bees and wasps can give you a bad _____.

(c) Airplanes, birds, and bees are _____s that can fly because they have _____s.

(d) When I broke my arm, the doctor put it in a _____.

(e) Don't leave your book at school, _____ it home.

2. **Pop and Snap**

(a) Use the clues and the beginning letters. Write words that end in **ap** and **op**.

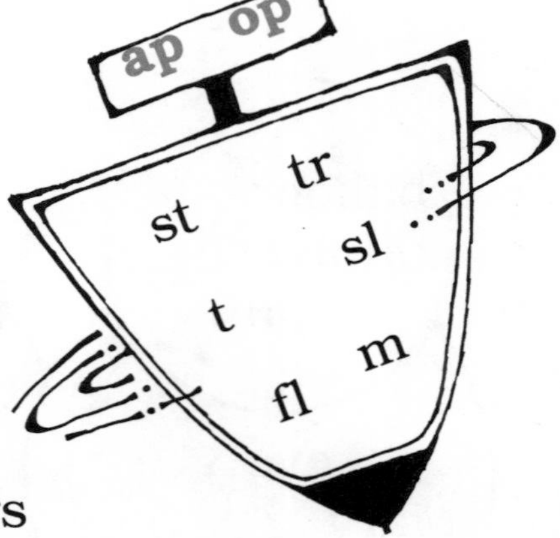

ap words	**op** words
(1) to catch	(4) to end
(2) hit	(5) spinning toy
(3) move wings	(6) to clean floors

(b) Write two other **ap** words and two other **op** words.

3. **Double a Letter**

Some words need to double the last letter before **ed** can be added. For example:

hop—hopped

(a) Add **ed** to: hug pop snap flip

(b) Use each new word in a sentence.

Writing Connections

1. **Box Word Rings**

Finish this word ring in your notebook.

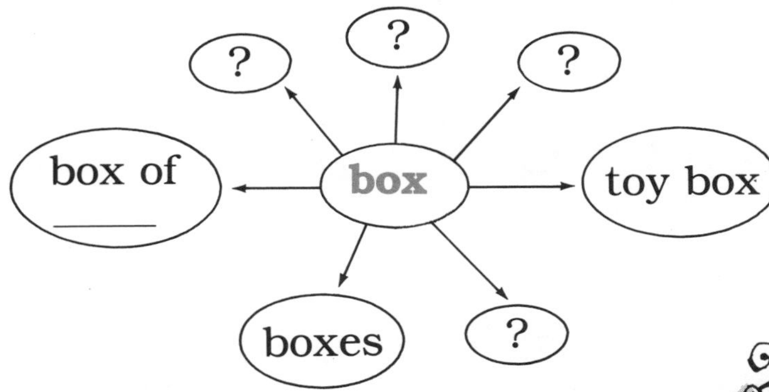

2. **Sounds Good!**

Write two or three sentences about something you like that **rings**, **pops**, or **snaps**.

Checkup
Add any problem words to your Personal Spelling Dictionary.

20 Valentines

if	read	bell	was	were	like
be	give	sad	mad	love	

Your Class Words

Add two or three more words to your list.

Checking What You Know

Use the Study Steps to learn new words.

Meaning Connections

1. **Valentine Rhymes**

   Can you _____ these valentine lines?

   Finish each rhyme. Use List Words.

Yes, I ____ all of them.

Pattern Connections

1. **Tell All**

(a) Write an **ell** word to match each clue.

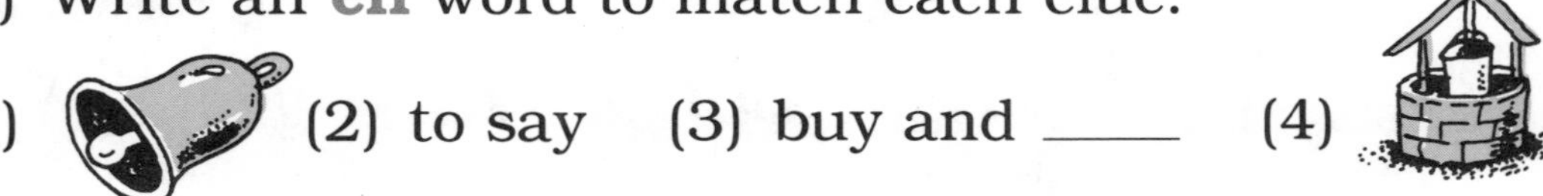

(1) (2) to say (3) buy and ____ (4)

(5) turtle's home

(b) Write an **all** word to match each clue.

(1) (2) shout (3) high (4) trip

(5) Humpty's "chair"

2. **If I Was...**

Choose **was** or **were**. Finish each sentence in your notebook.

(a) The two red valentines ____...

(b) One pretty valentine ____...

(c) The poems ____...

(d) A silver bell ____...

3. **E-X-P-L-O-D-I-N-G Words**

You can "explode" **like** by adding letters to the end to make new words:

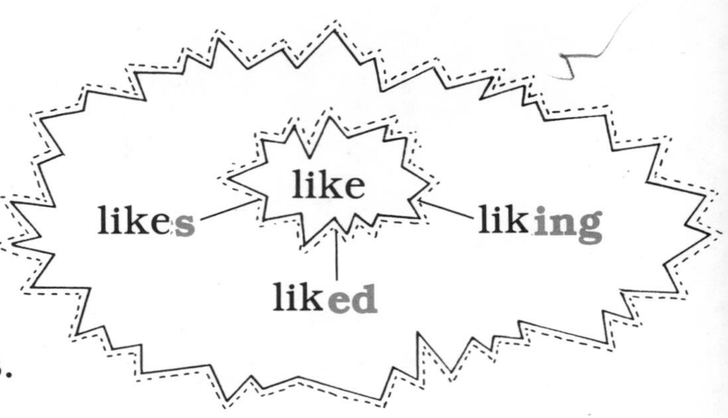

Add ending letters to E-X-P-L-O-D-E these words.

(a) love (b) hope (c) take (d) read

Writing Connections

1. **Be My Valentine**

Make a valentine card for a friend. Write a message for your card like the one shown.

An exclamation mark (!) is used to end a sentence that shows strong feeling.

You may wish to add exclamation marks to some of your valentine messages.

Checkup

Write in your Personal Spelling Dictionary any words you missed.

21 The Cookie Jar

jar	chip	seven	ten	four	box
saw	time	nine	six	five	

Your Class Words

Add more words your class would like to spell.

Checking What You Know

How many of the words do you already know?

Meaning Connections

1. **The Cookie Caper**

Read the story. Write List Words to finish it.

Early Sunday morning, Mrs. Brown checked the cookie jar. She _____ seven cookies.

At _____ o'clock, there were only _____ cookies. There was an empty milk glass in the sink.

At two o'clock, there were only five cookies in the cookie _____. There were fingerprints on the cupboard.

continued on the next page...

At _____ o'clock, there were four cookies left. Mrs. Brown found cookie crumbs all over the kitchen floor.

At _____ o'clock, only two cookies were left. No one wanted dessert.

At _____ o'clock, the kitchen floor creaked. Then there was only one cookie left.

On Monday morning, Mrs. Brown checked the cookie jar. It was empty.

Pattern Connections

1. **Exciting Boxes**

   (a) Write words that have an **x** to name each picture.

   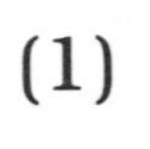

   (1)  _ _ _

   (3)  _ _ _

   (2)  _ _ _ _

   (4)  _ _ _

   (b) To make words that end in **x** mean more than one, you add **es** instead of just **s**.
   Make each of these words mean more than one:

   box six fox tax

   (c) Use two of your **es** words in a sentence.

2. **Time to Cross a Rhyme**

Copy the shapes. Add letters to make pairs of words that rhyme. Your List Words will help you.

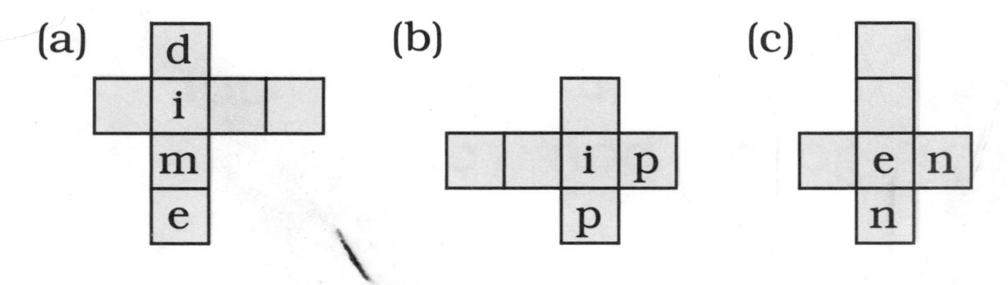

3. **An Awful Jawful**

Find the **aw** words that complete the sentences.

(a) You can cut wood with a _ aw.

(b) Lions' fingernails are called _ _ aw_.

(c) To make a picture you _ _ aw.

(d) You sip your drink with a _ _ _ aw.

Writing Connections

1. **Who Did It?**

Tell who ate the cookies in "The Cookie Caper."

2. **More Mystery**

Write a story about something that disappears. Tell when things happened and what clues were left.

▶ Check your spelling and punctuation.

Checkup

How many of your words can you spell now?

22 Hold It, Please!

cup stay cook hit fish pot
jam play gave pan drop

Your Class Words

Pick three more words you would like to learn.

Checking What You Know

Always use the Study Steps on page 11.

Meaning Connections

1. **Pots and Pans**

Finish this rhyming poem. Write in your notebook the List Words that fit.

What might you see in a ____?
Flowers? Soup? Or a knot?

What looks good on a dish?
A bear? A coat? Or a ____?

What can you drink from a ____?
Hot chocolate? Jam? Or a pup?

What do you ____ in a ____?
Roses, eggs, or a fan?

Pattern Connections

1. **Before You Cook**

   (a) Where would you **look** for a recipe? To find out, complete this rhyming poem.

   Write words that end with **ook**. When you are done, the circled letters will spell the answer to the riddle question.

   As I fished by a (b)r_ _ _,
   With a line and a h(_)_ _,
   My bait the fish t_(_)_,
   Now there's dinner
   to c_ _(_)!

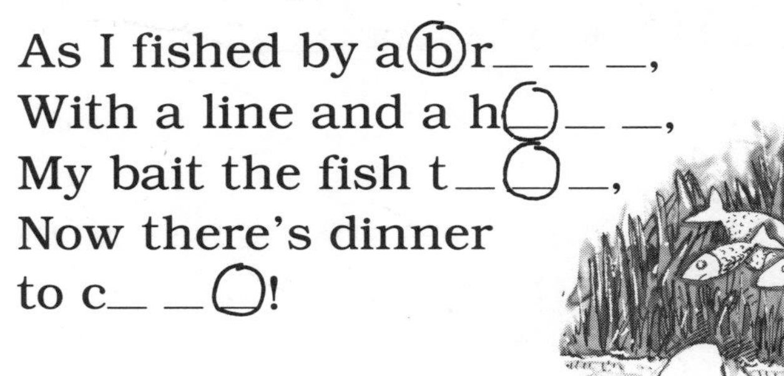

   (b) Write two more **ook** words you know.

   (c) Use two **ook** words in a rhyme or riddle.

2. **Tug on a Mug**

   Make new words. Change only **one** letter at a time. The arrows tell you which letters to change. Some words are done for you.

(a) m u g	r u g	r u n	f u n
(b) p o p	_ _ _	h o t	_ _ _
(c) s i t	_ _ _	h i d	_ _ _
(d) f a r	_ _ _	c a n	_ _ _
(e) h a m	_ _ _	_ _ _	c a r
(f) t r a p	t r i p	_ _ _ _	_ _ _ _

3. **Play With a**

Many words have the **a** sound in **way** or **save**.

(a) Copy the chart.

(b) Write the List Words that fit.

(c) Add two more words under each heading.

_ay	a_e
way	save

Writing Connections

1. **Have and Hold**

A bottle can hold water, juice, or a message. Write two or three things each of these can hold:

(a) a cup (b) a suitcase (c) a bowl (d) a bag

2. **Please Do Not Open**

What do you think is in the chest? Why is there a lock? Write at least three sentences to tell what is inside.

Commas (,) separate words in a list. Like this:

There were cups, pots, and pans in the sink.

Have you used commas correctly?

Checkup

Use your Personal Spelling Dictionary. Add any problem words.

23 Pet Tricks

boy	dog	bed
girl	say	bring
see	ran	come
I'm	can't	play

Your Class Words

Are there any other words you'd like to spell?

Checking What You Know

Pay special attention to any words you had trouble with.

Meaning Connections

1. **Barkly**

(a) Read the story to see how smart Mitsu's pet Barkly is.

My dog Barkly is a good pet. When he runs toward me, I say, "Come, Barkly. Run, Barkly. What a good dog!"

When Barkly wants treats, he comes to me. Sometimes he sits and begs. I say, "Sit, Barkly. Beg, Barkly. What a smart dog!"

continued on the next page...

Barkly likes to chew my slippers. When he sees me coming, he drops them. I say, "No, boy. Stop that." Then I pat Barkly's head to show I'm not angry.

Sometimes Barkly brings me his blanket. I say, "Good boy. I see you're tired." Then I fix his bed.

It's fun to train a dog like Barkly.

(b) Write all the commands that Barkly obeyed.
For example: "Run, Barkly."

(c) In the story, **them** is used to replace the word **slippers**.
Write **all** the List Words that could be replaced by each of these words:

(1) she (2) he (3) it

Pattern Connections

1. **Into the Doghouse**

Compound words are made with two small words. Like this:

in + **to** = into

Write compound words. Use **dog**, **play**, or **bed** with each of the words in the doghouse.

(a) dog + _____ = ?
(b) play + _____ = ?
(c) play + _____ = ?
(d) play + _____ = ?
(e) bed + _____ = ?
(f) bed + _____ = ?

2. **"Add s!"**

(a) Add **s** to **see**, **say**, **come**, **bring**, and **play**. Write the new words.

(b) Use any **three** of the new words in sentences.

3. **Word Shrinkers**

Some words, like **he's** and **you're**, are short forms called **contractions**.

Write the short forms for:

(a) I am
(b) can not
(c) did not
(d) it is
(e) that is
(f) do not

Writing Connections

1. **On Command**

People need to obey commands, too. Write a command you might see

(a) on a lawn.
(b) in a library.
(c) on a stoplight.
(d) near a dangerous place.

2. **Human Tricks**

Barkly trained his owner to fix his bed. Barkly did it by bringing her his blanket.
Write a few sentences about how Barkly might teach his owner another trick.

Checking What You Know
Did you learn any new "spelling tricks"?

24 Backup

boy	pop	ten	give	bed
girl	gun	nine	gave	by
five	say	pot	love	see
four	ran	pan	bring	saw
be	jam	read	dog	time
box	jar	book	cup	your
play	I'm	cook	fish	gum
stay	can't	hit	chip	come
was	drop	sad	bell	orange
were	six	mad	like	use
if	seven	ring	snap	

1. **Reach for the Sky**

Build the tallest ladder you can. Try to reach the Blue Sky. Drop **two** letters from a List Word to make new words. For each new word you write, climb one step on your ladder.

2. **Word Stairs**

Now, build some stairs. Use the last letter of a List Word to start a new List Word. Like this:

```
s n a p
      o
      p l a y
```

3. **Hink-Pinks**

A **hink-pink** is a riddle with two rhyming words for an answer. Like this:

What do you call a guppy plate? a fish dish

(a) Use List Words and other words to complete each hink-pink:

(1) Where could you buy soda? at a p_____ _____

(2) What's a rosy place to sleep? a red _____

(3) Where does the beekeeper go after number four? to hive _____

(4) What do you call an unhappy father? a _____ dad

(5) What's the opposite of a work night? a _____ day

(6) What do you call a mug for a young dog? a pup _____

(7) What's a silly name for a bell? a r_____ th_____

(b) Make up two of your own hink-pinks. Trade them with a classmate.

4. Puniddles

A **puniddle** is a pair of pictures that suggest a compound word. Write the words for these puniddles. For example:

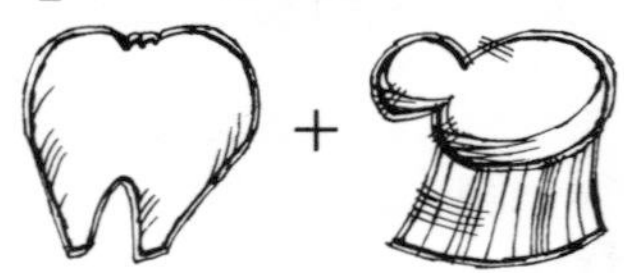

tooth **brush** = toothbrush

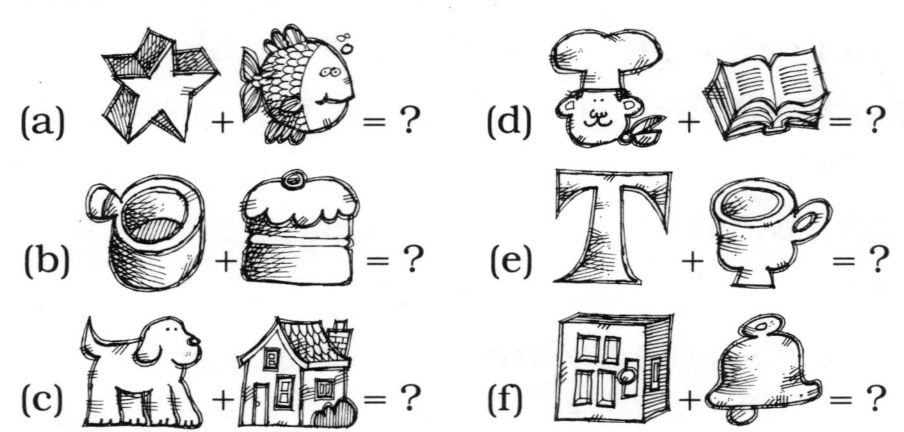

5. One to One

Find the List Word that completes each sentence puzzle. Write the completed sentences in your notebook. Like this:

Good is to **bad** as **happy** is to sad.

(a) **Is** is to **are** as **was** is to _____.

(b) **Lose** is to **find** as **take** is to _____.

(c) **Four** is to **eight** as **three** is to _____.

(d) **Tea** is to **pot** as **cookie** is to _____.

(e) **Air** is to **bird** as **water** is to _____.

(f) **Bark** is to **dog** as **ring** is to _____.

(g) **Will** is to **won't** as **can** is to _____.

Wordworks

1. **Number Rhymes**

   Write number rhymes. Pick some numbers, in order, and make up a rhyme. Like this:

   One, two —
"Get the glue!"

   Three, four —
"Cover the floor!"

2. **Exploding Number Sentences**

   Explode each number sentence. Like this:

(number)	(thing)	(doing)	(when, where, or how)
One	son	is playing	just for fun.
	bun	is cooking	in the sun.
	drum	is beating	rum-tum-tum.

Two _____ are _____ _____.
_____ _____ _____.
_____ _____ _____.

Three _____ _____ _____.
_____ _____ _____.
_____ _____ _____.

Five _____ _____ _____.
_____ _____ _____.
_____ _____ _____.

▶ Trade sentences with a partner. Check each other's spelling.

25 Missing

as	fill	now	why	miss	Dad
top	big	add	wish	it	out

Your Class Words

Choose three more words to add to your list.

Checking What You Know
How many of your words can you already spell?

Meaning Connections

1. **Triple Trouble**

   (a) Read the poem "Triple Trouble."

   My top two teeth are missing.
   Dad calls me "Funny Face!"
   And when I bite an apple,
   It fills the big, wide space.

   One bottom tooth is missing.
   Now that adds up to three.
   And when I blow a bubble,
   It's as odd as it can be!

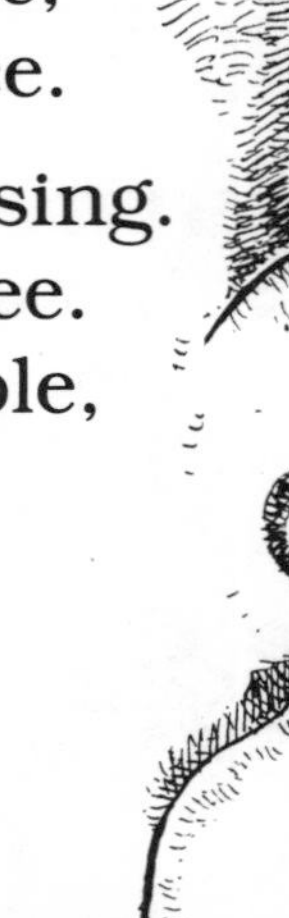

(b) Write the List Word in the poem that

(1) is the opposite of **bottom**.

(2) rhymes with **has**.

(3) is the opposite of **subtracts**.

(4) rhymes with **fit**.

(5) is the opposite of **small**.

(6) means "father."

Pattern Connections

1. **It's Out Now!**

(a) Write the List Words that have the same **ou** sound as **how** or **ouch**.

(b) Use the **ow** or **ou** spelling pattern to complete these words:

GRRRRRRR.

_ _ _ e l   f _ _ _ n   g r _ _ _

_ _ _ s _   _ _ _ t h

(c) Use two **ow** or **ou** words in a rhyming verse. Like this:

There really isn't any doubt,
That little tooth must come out.

2. **Which One?**

(a) Make two headings in your notebook:

w	wh

Write the List Words that begin with **w** and **wh**.

(b) Write four other words under each heading.

3. **Brushup**

You can make a word "grow" by adding letters to the beginning or end to make new words:

brush brushes, brushing, brusher, brushed

Make these words "grow": **fill** **miss**

Writing Connections

1. **Three Wishes**

If you were granted **three** wishes, what would you wish for? Write sentences to tell what you would wish.

2. **Feeling Lost**

Write about how you felt when you lost your first tooth. Tell how it came out and what you did with it.

Checkup

Write in your Personal Spelling Dictionary any words you had trouble with.

26 Send in the Clowns

name	hat	children
clown	other	chin
circus	foot	has
coat	long	surprise

Your Class Words

Choose three more words your class would like to spell.

Checking What You Know

Don't forget the Study Steps. See page 11.

Meaning Connections

1. **Under the Big Top**

Write the List Words that finish this story.

My n___ is Chuck and I work in the Big Top C___. Before each show, I paint on a happy face. Then I pop on my orange wig and my tall h___.

Next, I slip into my costume. It h___ a big collar and l___ baggy pants. I also wear a silly red c___. Last, I pull on my floppy shoes—first one f___, and then the o___.

S___! Here comes Bozo, the funny circus c___.

Pattern Connections

1. **Clap for the Clowns**

   (a) Look at the clown hats. Clip a **cl** beginning onto the word endings on each hat. Use two word endings of your own.

   (b) See how many **cl** words you can use in a sentence.

2. **A Cheerful Chap**

   (a) Write the List Words that begin with **ch**.

   (b) Use the picture clues to find the missing parts of these **ch** words. Write the words in your notebook.

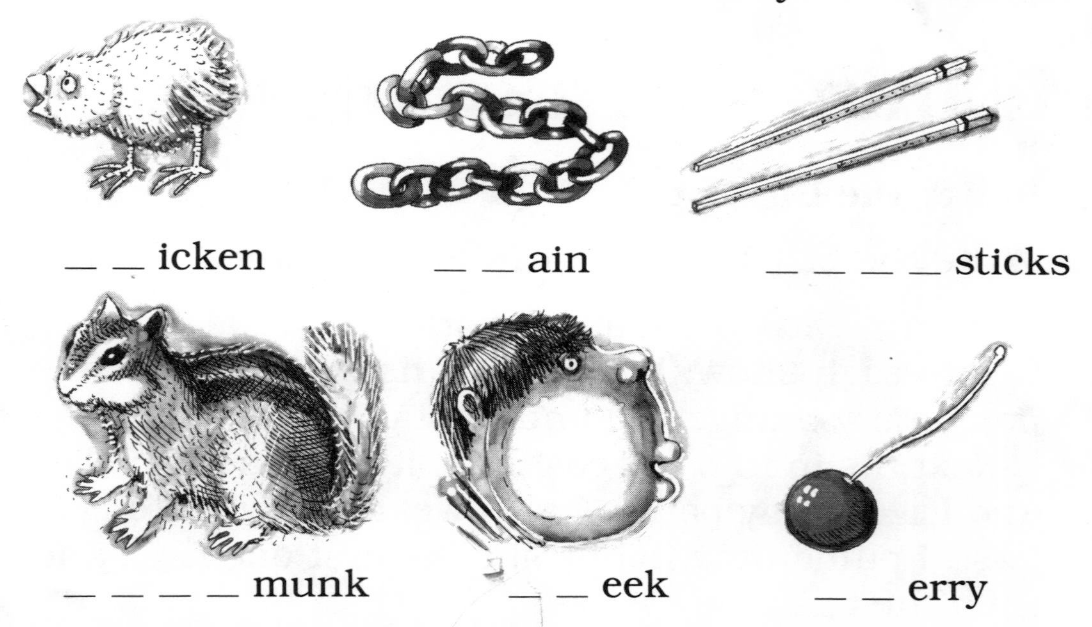

   (c) See how many other **ch** words you can write.

3. **A Juggling Act**

Chuck picked out different letters from this word and juggled them around.
Here are some words he wrote:

cow no low now won
own snow slow

Write as many small words as you can using the letters in these words.
(a) children (b) surprise

Writing Connections

1. **Circus Acts**

Chuck was a clown in the Big Top Circus. What would you like to be if you could join the circus?

Write a story to tell what you would wear and what you would do in the Big Top Circus.

▶ Reread your story. Could some of the short sentences be joined by using words such as **and**, **but**, **or**, **when**, and **because**?

Checkup

See how many of your words you can spell now.

27 Animal Fables

mouse	lion	after	stop
friends	told	came	how
from	them	sleep	they

Your Class Words

Add three more words to your list.

Checking What You Know

Write the correct spelling of any word you didn't know. Underline the letters you found difficult.

Meaning Connections

1. **The Mouse's Squeak**

Read this fable. Then, write the List Words you could use instead of the words printed **like this**.

Mouse and Lion were **pals**. Mouse felt safe with **the king of the jungle** by his side. Each evening, Lion roared and all the animals would **end** their fighting. Then Lion and Mouse could go to **bed**.

One evening, Mouse began to squeak. He squeaked until the animals **ran** to see what was wrong. Mouse **asked** all of **the animals** to get along with one another. The animals agreed.

From that day on, all the jungle animals were friendly to each other.

Lesson: It's not how loud you speak, it's what you say that matters.

Pattern Connections

1. **Ants, Birds, and Cats**

   Write the List Words in **abc** order.

(1) ____	(4) fro____	(7) ____	(10) the____
(2) ____	(5) ____	(8) sl____	(11) the____
(3) fri____	(6) ____	(9) st____	(12) to____

2. **Free as a Bird**

   (a) Write the List Words that begin with **fr**.

   (b) Write three other **fr** words.

   (c) Use one of your **fr** words to write a lesson a fable could teach. Like this:

   Nothing in life is free.

3. **Sly as a Fox—Strong as an Ox**

Add **sl** or **st** to the word endings. Write a new word that completes each phrase.

(a) _____ as a snail

(b) _____ in the mud (d) _____ in bed

(c) _____ on the ice (e) grocery _____ (f) a _____ sign

Writing Connections

1. **Make Your Own Fable**

Finish this fable. First, make the choices to tell what is happening. Then, write an ending. Write the lesson the fable teaches.

Two [ducks / turtles] were walking to the pond to [have a swim / have a picnic.]. On the way, they met a [friendly / mean] fox.

"On your way to the pond?" he asked.

"Oh, yes, we [go every day / have never been there]," said the friends.

The fox [smiled / scowled]. "Then, let me...

Checkup

See how many List Words you can spell now.

28 A Dream Pony

cow	pony	grow
hay	ride	birthday
star	feed	father
farm	fine	happy

Your Class Words

Add words your class would like to spell.

Checking What You Know

Don't forget to use the Study Steps every day.

Meaning Connections

1. **Lisa's Dream**

Write the List Words that finish this story.

Lisa lived on a ____. Every day she did her chores. She saved all the money she earned. She dreamed of having her own ____ to ____.

Her neighbour had a beautiful black foal. Lisa had watched the pony ____ bigger and stronger each day. How she wished it could be hers!

One morning she went to ____ the chickens. There

continued on the next page...

in the yard was the pony, munching on some ____.
Lisa couldn't believe her eyes. Then she heard her ____ call from the barn.

"____ ____, Lisa! How do you like your present?"

Pattern Connections

1. **Riding Double**

   (a) Join a List Word with each of these words—**house**, **yard**, **bell**, **stack**, **hide**, **loft**, **land**—to make new words. Like this:

   farm + **land** = farmland

   (b) Use three of the new compound words to write sentences about the picture.

2. **Horse Before the Cart**

   (a) Write the two List Words with the **ar** pattern.

   (b) The pony is pulling a c**ar**t of **ar** things. Write the **ar** words. Add two **ar** words of your own.

3. **Silent (e) Ranch**

(a) These ponies were just bought by the Silent (e) Ranch. Add an e to the word on each pony. Write the new words in your notebook.

(b) Take a ride on one of the ponies. Write a sentence using the word before **and** after you added e. Like this:

To get rid of my anger, I go for a pony ride.

Writing Connections

1. **Farm Animals**

A **horse** is an animal you might find on a farm. Make a list of other animals that are raised on a farm.

2. **A Pony of Your Own**

Would you like your own pony? What would you feed it? Where would you ride it?

Write a story about what you would do if you had a pony. Give your pony a name.

▶ Trade stories. Check each other's spelling.

Checkup

Write in your Personal Spelling Dictionary any words you missed.

29 Home Sweet Home

bug	story	milk	town	house	night
dish	clock	city	zoo	rug	mouse

Your Class Words

Choose three more words to add to your list.

Checking What You Know

Write the correct spelling of any words you didn't know.

Meaning Connections

1. **House Guests**

(a) Read the poem to find out what each thing calls "home."

People can live in houses,
A bug makes its home in a rug.
A dish makes its home in a cupboard,
And milk can be found in a jug.

A book is a home for a story,
A clock is the place for time.
A song is the home for a tune,
And this poem's a place for a rhyme.

(b) List all of the **things** in the poem. List all of their **homes**. Do it in a chart like this:

Things	**Their homes**
people	houses

(c) Add two other things and their homes.

Pattern Connections

1. **A Nice Place**

(a) Write the List Word and three other words that have the **c** sound as in **ice**.

(b) Use two of your **c** words in sentences about homes.

2. **Room for All**

(a) Write the List Word that has the same vowel sound as **too**.

(b) Finish this poem. All the missing words have the same vowel sound as **too**.

Soup can be found on a ,

Air fills up a 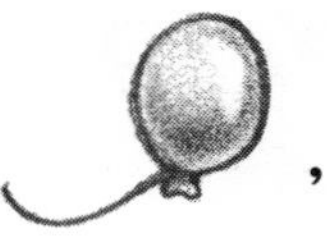,

A witch may ride on a ,

And the sky is home for the .

3. **The House of Clocks**

(a) Use the beginning letters on the clock to write words with the **ock** spelling pattern.

(b) Write your own words for the other hours.

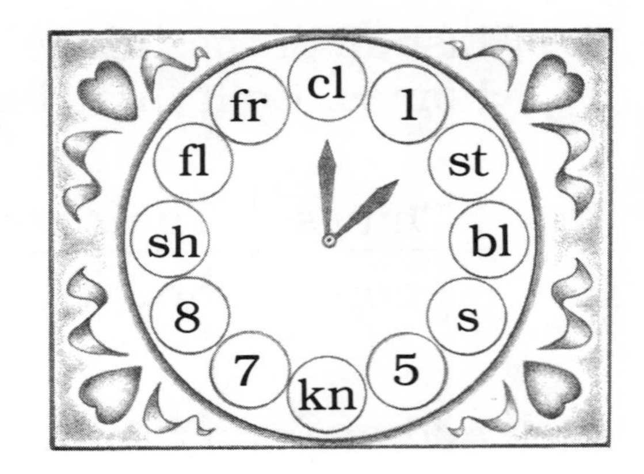

Writing Connections

1. **A House in Town**

Use each pair of words to write a sentence.

(a) house town (b) city night (c) dish milk

2. **Where Is Home?**

What could live in a mitten? Where could the colour orange find a home?

Make up your own poem about where different things might find a home.

Checkup

See how many words you can spell now.

Backup

add	it	star	clown	now
Dad	rug	them	top	city
grow	happy	has	town	lion
coat	cow	as	feed	other
why	story	they	sleep	big
hay	friends	stop	surprise	house
told	children	mouse	out	father
chin	dish	milk	farm	circus
bug	ride	after	how	miss
night	came	fill	name	zoo
from	long	clock	pony	fine
foot	wish	birthday	hat	

1. **Scrambled Questions**

Unscramble the List Words in each question and write them in your notebook. Then answer the question by writing **Yes** or **No**. Like this:

Can you read a **ortys**? story — Yes

(a) Does the moon shine at **ghnit**?

(b) Can you **edfe** a saw?

(c) Can you wish on a **tasr**?

(d) Can you **idre** a **noyp**?

(e) Can you **ilmk** a **esuom**?

2. Magic Squares

In these squares, the first and last letter of each word is also the first or last letter of another word.

c	o	w
a		h
t	o	y

p	o	o	l
o			o
n			u
y	a	r	d

Copy the following squares. Use the clues to complete each square. The arrows show which way to print each word.

(a) (1)↓ (2)↓

	(1)↓		(2)↓
(3)→	h		t
(4)→	s		p

(b)

	(1)↓			(2)↓
(3)→	f			m
(4)→				

(c)

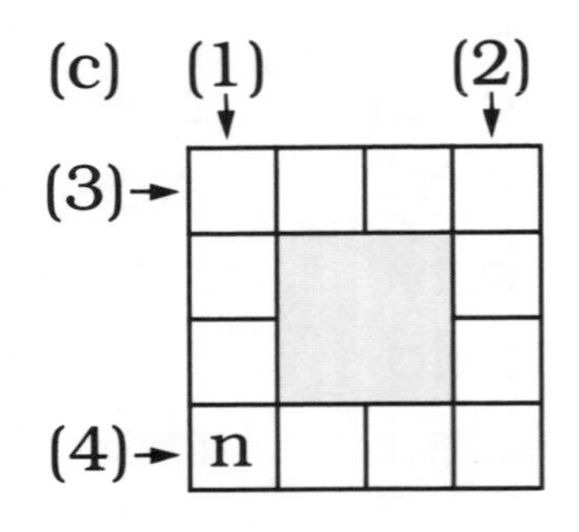

(a) (1) I have, she ____.
(2) not the bottom but the ____
(3) a covering for your head
(4) the juice in a tree

(b) (1) the end of a leg
(2) it shines at night
(3) the opposite of **to**
(4) a small city

(c) (1) in a short time
(2) go for a pony ____
(3) it twinkles at night
(4) used to call someone

3. **Take It Away**

There are **two** List Words hidden in each group of letters. Use the clues to take away the letters of **one** List Word. The letters that are left will spell the other List Word. Write both words. Like this:

Take away the **time** but leave the **words**.

s c t l o o r c y k clock — story

(a) Take away the **little horse** but leave its **food**.

p h a o y n y

(b) Take away the **big town** but leave the **twinkle**.

c s i t t a y r

(c) Take away the **Big Top** but leave the **tricks**.

c l c o i r w c u n s

4. **On the Opposite Foot**

Make an opposite shoe for Bozo the Clown by writing the opposite List Words. One is done for you.

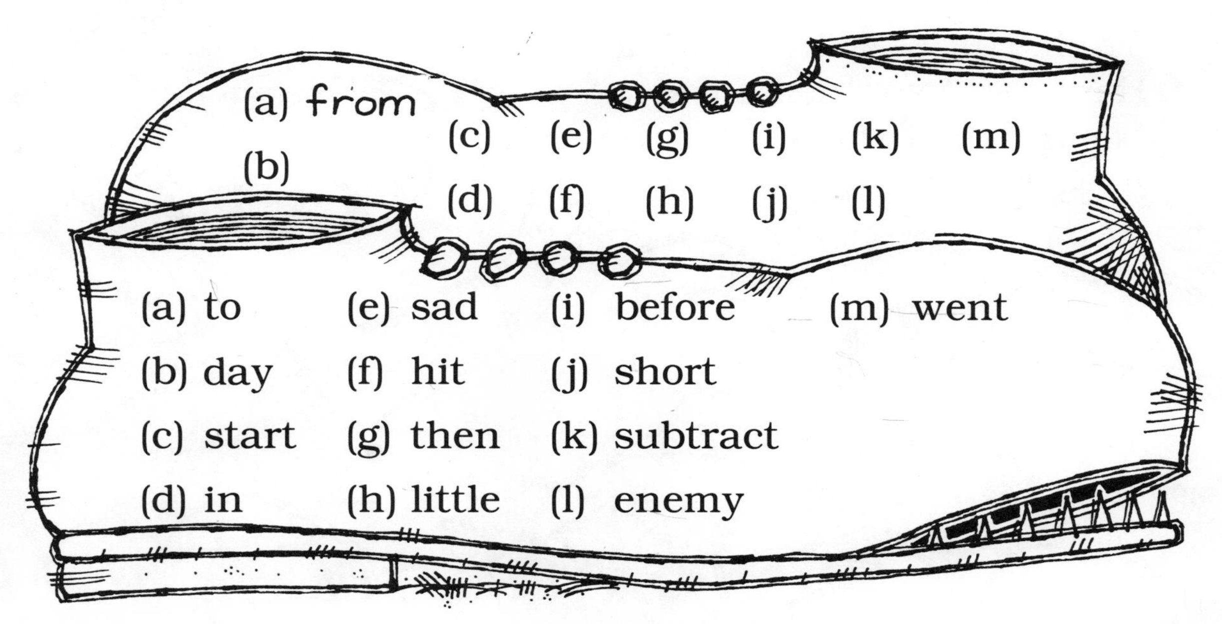

Wordworks

1. **I Wish...**

Imagine you find a genie in a bottle! The genie grants you three wishes.

Use **three** of the sentence starters below to write about the wishes you ask for.

I wish [I could... / I was... / I had... / that... / I didn't have to...] because... [____. / ____. / ____.]

2. **A Wish Come True**

Imagine that something you wished for came true. How would you feel? How would your friends feel? What would be different in your life? Write a story to tell about what would happen.

▶ Trade stories with a partner. How could you make the beginning of the story more interesting?

31 Crowns

man lived king
had gold thank
who this crown
too kind there
upon

Your Class Words

Think of three more words you'd like to spell.

Checking What You Know

Did you spell all of the words correctly?

Meaning Connections

1. **Fit for a King**

   Write the List Words that complete this story.

   Once _____ a time, there _____ a wise, old king who had no children. The king wanted to find someone _____ would wear his golden crown and rule his kingdom wisely.

   People came from near and far to try on the golden _____.

continued on the next page...

One said, "_____ makes me look handsome."
"This will surely make me a grand _____," said another.
At last, a fine young _____ appeared. "Might I try on the crown of gold, _____?" he asked. "If I could be as wise and as _____ as you," he said, "then surely I would not need a crown to be king. I _____ you, Sire."
"You have spoken wisely," said the king. "The crown of _____ will be yours!"

Pattern Connections

1. **Crown Jewels**

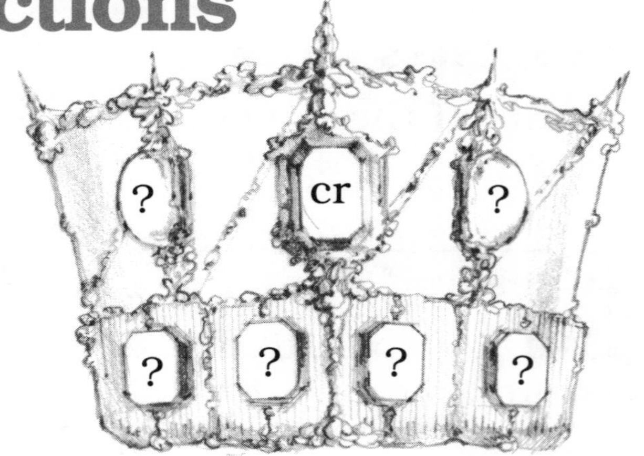

(a) Make words that have the **own** pattern as in **down**. Write one word for each jewel on the crown.

(b) Make up a rhyme using **own** words.

2. **It's on My Mind**

Solve the king's puzzle. Write words with the **ind** pattern as in **mind**.

(a) opposite of **cruel**
(b) to twist and turn
(c) at the back
(d) cannot see
(e) opposite of **losing**

(a)				i	n	d			
(b)			w						
(c)	b	e							
(d)				i	n	d			
(e)				i	n	d	i	n	g

3. **This Crown, That Crown**

The king went to his crownmaker to buy a new crown. Find out what he decided to buy. Write the **th** words that finish this poem.

_____ one here is old, _____ one there is new.
_____ ones here are fine, _____ ones there won't do.
On second thought, I'll take _____ all,
For _____ will be a Royal Ball.

Writing Connections

1. **Crowned With**...

Kings and queens wear crowns on their heads. Write sentences about four other special things people wear on their heads. Tell why. Like this:

Skiers wear toques to keep their ears warm.

Checkup
Add any problem words to your Personal Spelling Dictionary.

32 Getting There

jet	boat	train
bus	want	truck
way	dark	yellow
car	fast	try
didn't	will	

Your Class Words

There are lots of "travel" words. Add two to your list.

Checking What You Know

Did you miss any words? The Study Steps will help.

Meaning Connections

1. **The Way to Go**

(a) Read the poem to find a great way to travel.

I want to travel to a faraway land,
To see dark jungles and bright yellow sand.
There are so many places I want to know.
I wonder which way is the best to go...
By car or boat or passenger train?
By bus or truck or a fast jet plane?
There's only one sure way I know:
A book will take me where I want to go.

(b) Write the names of all the vehicles in the poem.

(c) Write the List Word that means the opposite of

(1) won't (2) slow (3) light (4) did

Pattern Connections

1. **Keep Afloat**

(a) Write the List Word that has the **oat** pattern.

(b) Write new **oat** words. Use the beginning letters **g**, **c**, **fl**, and **thr**.

(c) Use your **oat** words. Write sentences that tell if these things **can** or **can't** float. Like this:
A throat can't float.

2. **Travel the Trail**

(a) Write the List Words that begin with **tr**.

(b) Travel the trail. Print new **tr** words using the letters shown. Add **three** more **tr** words.

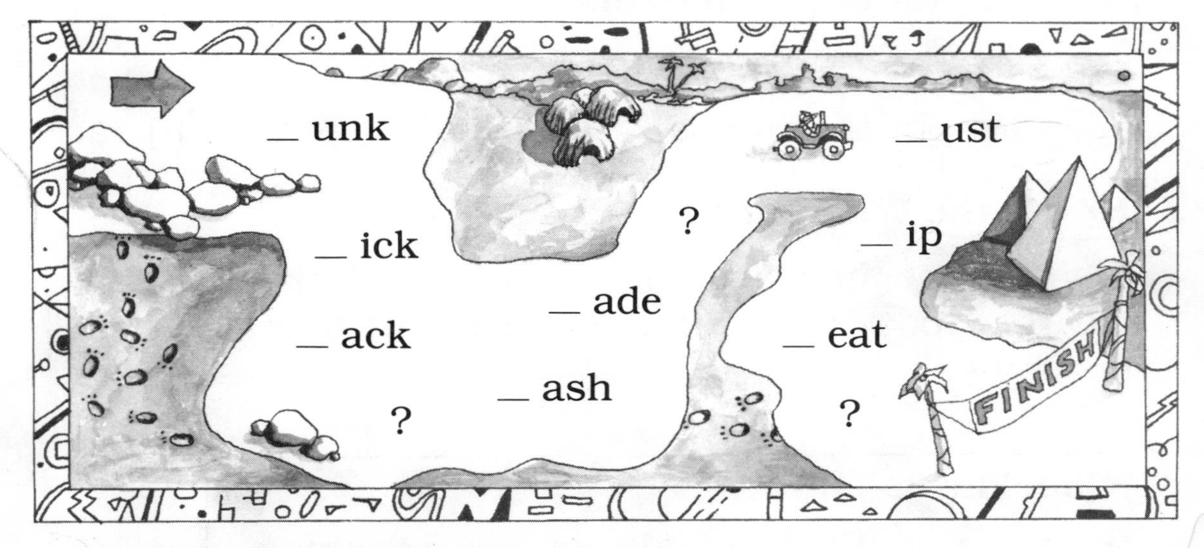

(c) Use three **tr** words in sentences.

3. **Travel Forecast**

Use these beginning letters with the **ast** spelling pattern. Complete the travel weather report.

l bl p f

(a) Icy winds will _____ the city.

(b) A _____ drop in temperature may bring snow.

(c) The storm should _____ until evening.

(d) That's the third storm in the _____ week.

Writing Connections

1. **Travelling, and How!**

How would you travel in these ways? Write a sentence for each. Like this:

I could steer a bumper car.

(a) ride (b) fly (c) sail (d) pedal (e) pull (f) race

2. **How's the Weather?**

Would someone travelling to your area enjoy the weather today? Write a weather report telling why or why not.

Checkup

How many of your words can you spell now?

33 Mud Puddles

black	soft	glad	wet	blue
walk	cake	rain	step	
mud	skip	kick	jump	

Your Class Words

Are there any other words you'd like to add?

Checking What You Know

Write any words you spelled incorrectly.
Underline the letters you found difficult.

Meaning Connections

1. **Mud Fun**

(a) Read the poem to find out what is fun about mud.

We like to walk in mud,
Ishy, squishy mud.
It's cool and wet and black,
And leaves a gooey track.

We like to play in mud,
Icky, sticky mud.
We make a cake outdoors,
We're glad it rains and pours.

(b) Write the List Word that means

(1) happy
(2) falling water drops
(3) soft, wet earth
(4) a sweet bread

(c) **Soft** and **oozy** are two words you can use to describe mud. Write the words in the poem used to describe mud.

(d) Write three other words that could describe mud.

Pattern Connections

1. **A Black Blob**

(a) Make words by adding **bl** to the word endings. Use four word endings of your own.

bl + ew, ?, ade, ame, ue, ?, ?, oom, ack, ?, izzard

(b) Write a **tongue twister**. Use as many **bl** words as you can. Like this:

A black blob blotched my blue blazer.

2. **Oh So Soft**

Use the word beginnings in the footprints. Add them to the word endings in the chart to make new words. The clues will help you.

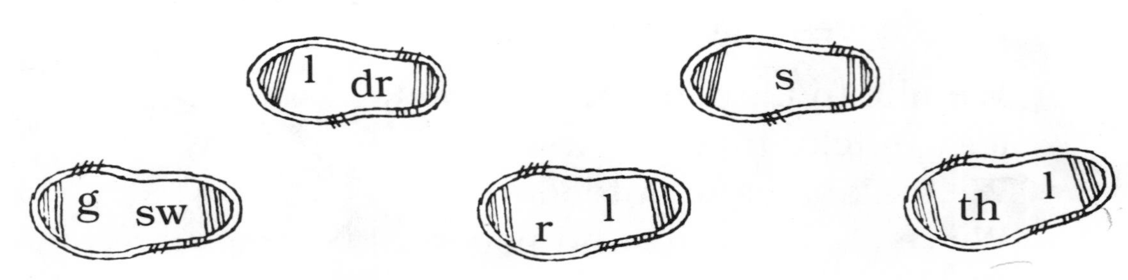

_ ift	_ oft	_ aft	_ eft
(a) pick up (b) a present (c) very fast	(d) not loud (e) hay ____	(f) blast of air (g) flat boat	(h) not right (i) stealing

3. **Then and Now**

Then: Yesterday I played in the rain.

Now: Today I play in the mud.

Copy this chart. Write the action words that show actions happening **now** or **then**.

Now	Then
walk	(a)
kick	(b)
(c)	skipped
jump	(d)
(e)	stepped

Writing Connections

1. **Rainy Day Fun**

It's Saturday. It's raining. You put on your raincoat and boots and go outside. Write a journal story about what you did. Like this:

My Journal Saturday, June 6

Today I played outside in the splashy rain. I...

Can you add any describing words to make your story more interesting?

Checkup

See how many words you can spell now.

34 Sandworks

need work end sand keep
let took dig take print
today away hill party

Your Class Words

Add words your class would like to spell.

Checking What You Know

Use the Study Steps to learn new words.

Meaning Connections

1. **Sand Play**

(a) Read this story about building with sand.

Take some sand and...

1. dig a hole
2. build a hill
3. keep it wet
4. work away
5. add more sand
6. smooth it out
7. take your time
   and end up with a...

(b) **Take** is an action word. Write the other action words used in "Sand Play."

2. **Sand Castle Secret**

What is buried in this sand castle? To find out, write in your notebook the List Words that complete the puzzle. Then read the letters in the word pole.

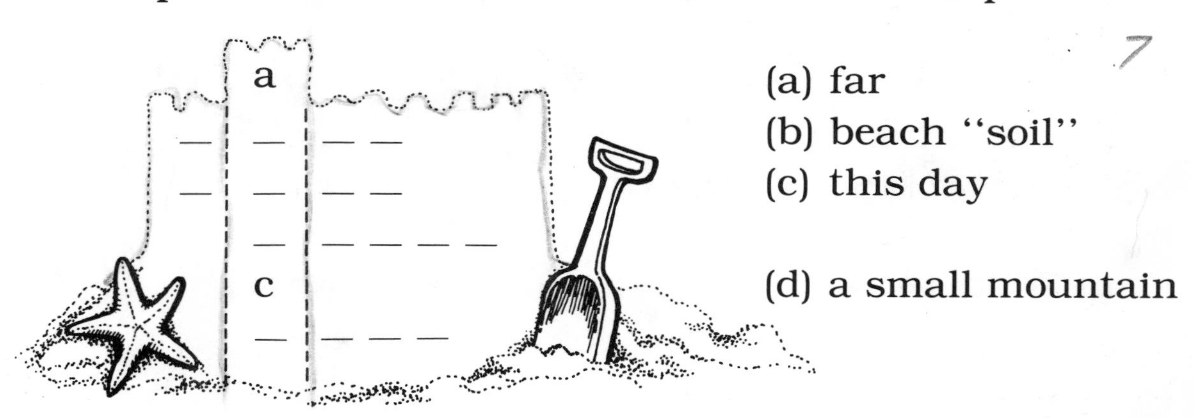

(a) far

(b) beach "soil"

(c) this day

(d) a small mountain

Pattern Connections

1. **I See You Saw It**

Copy the chart below. Write the words that show actions happening **now** and **then**. These action words do **not** add **ed** to show "then."

Now	Then
Today I...	**Yesterday I...**
sit	sat
take	(a)
(b)	dug
fall	(c)
(d)	kept

2. **Working With ing**

(a) You can make an action word grow by adding **ing**. Add **ing** to these action words.

let party keep take
work dig print need

Write them in a chart like this:

Just add **ing**	Drop final **e**, add **ing**	Double last letter, add **ing**
watering	making	sitting

(b) Write two sentences that use **ing** words.

Writing Connections

1. **Sand Sculptures**

Write a story telling how to build something out of sand. What would you need? What would you do first? What would you do next? What is the last thing you would do?

Exchange your story with a partner. Did your partner write all the steps in order?

Checkup

Don't forget to add any words you had trouble with to your Personal Spelling Dictionary.

35 Recipes for Family Fun

swim	most	grandmother	tag	small
baby	done	grandfather	rest	family
sister	green	pretty	park	

Your Class Words

Add three more words to your list.

Checking What You Know

Use the Study Steps every day to learn new words.

Meaning Connections

1. **Recipe for Summer Fun**

   Write the List Words that complete this recipe.

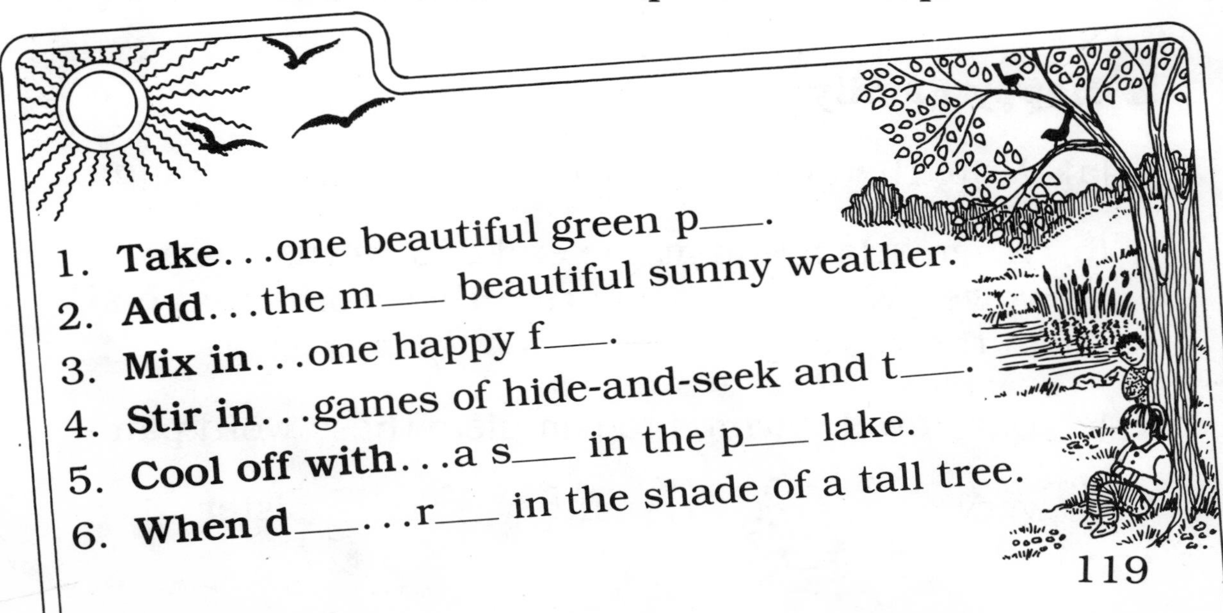

Pattern Connections

1. **Tag Along**

   (a) Use the clues to make words with the **ag** pattern. Write the words in your notebook.

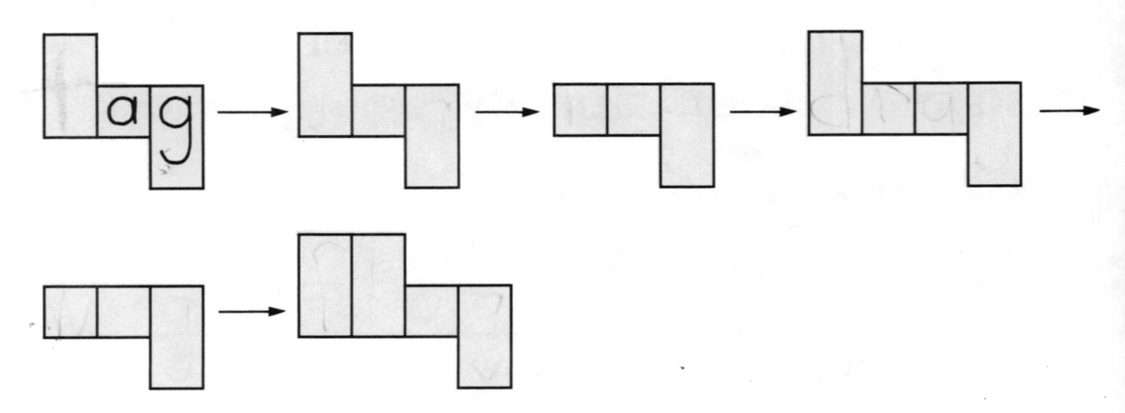

   (1) a game
   (2) a paper container
   (3) an old cloth
   (4) to pull
   (5) to move back and forth
   (6) a cloth that stands for a country

   (b) Use three of your **ag** words in a sentence.

2. **Happy Family**

   (a) Write the List Words with the **y** sound in **happy**.

   (b) When **y** is found at the end of a word, it is a vowel. Write at least three other words that end in the vowel **y**.

   (c) Use vowel **y** words to complete these word pairs:

   very _____ _____ weather _____ sister

3. **Smile Sweetly**

Use **sm** or **sw** with the patterns on the grapes. Write the new words. The clues will help you.

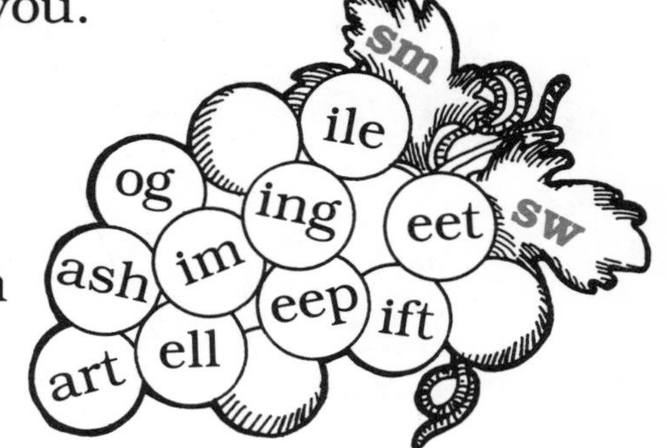

- fast
- clever
- to float
- to grin
- not sour
- to break
- to brush
- to sniff
- move back and forth
- smoke and fog

Writing Connections

1. **A Recipe for Fun**

Write your own recipe for **one** of these:

- a night of family fun at home
- a day at the park
- ways to keep busy on your holidays

2. **Family Snap Shots**

Draw a picture of each person in your family. Beside each picture, write one interesting thing about that person. Like this:

Grandmother

My grandmother takes me fishing.

Checkup

Can you spell all your words now?

36 Backup

jet	let	baby	small	crown
bus	wet	sister	upon	hill
fast	rain	this	lived	jump
car	today	yellow	work	step
truck	family	gold	take	soft
try	grandfather	too	took	cake
train	man	blue	away	keep
boat	who	kick	end	had
kind	didn't	pretty	rest	party
grandmother	done	park	tag	skip
black	print	dark	walk	there
mud	glad	swim	way	green
sand	will	want	thank	
dig	need	most	king	

1. Travelling Letters

Change only **one** letter in each of the words below to make new words. Like this:

dig big

Write the new words.

(a) jet	(d) kind	(g) will	(j) lived
(b) fast	(e) mud	(h) swim	(k) park
(c) car	(f) dig	(i) had	(l) too

2. **Magic Squares**

In Magic Squares, the first and last letter of each word is also the first or last letter of another word. Like this:

j	e	t
a		a
m	i	x

Copy the Magic Squares below. Use List Words to finish each square.

(a)

e		d
a		
t		

(b)

j		t
a		
w		o

(c)

		d
		a
n	o	d

(d)

l		
a		
w		

(e)

k			d
g	l	u	e

(f)

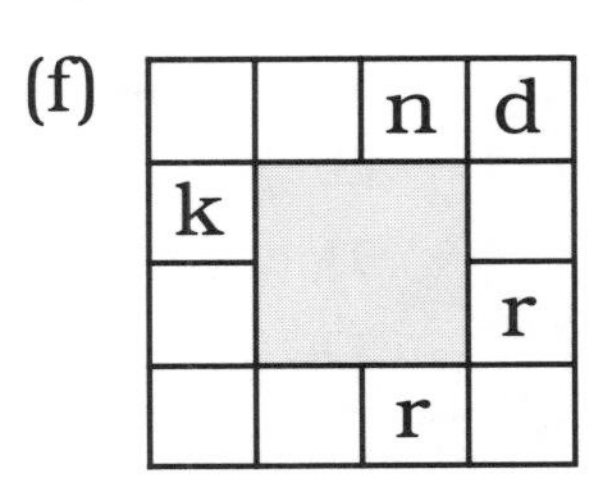

		n	d
k			
			r
		r	

(g)

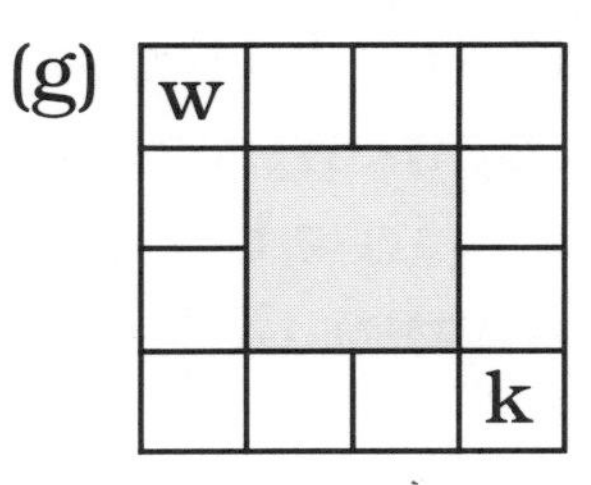

w			
			k

3. **Words That Go Together**

(a) Write List Words that go with **too** and **away** to make sentence parts. Like this:

too small take away

(b) Choose **three** of your sentence parts. Use each in a complete sentence. Like this:

The king's new crown was too small.

4. **Key Vowels**

Copy this chart. Complete it using List Words with the same vowel sounds as the "key" words.

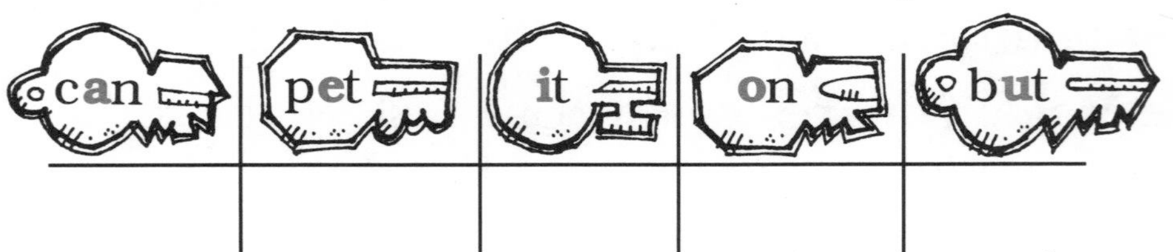

5. **Double Crown**

Find the List Words with double letters. Write them in your notebook in **abc** order. The crown will help you.

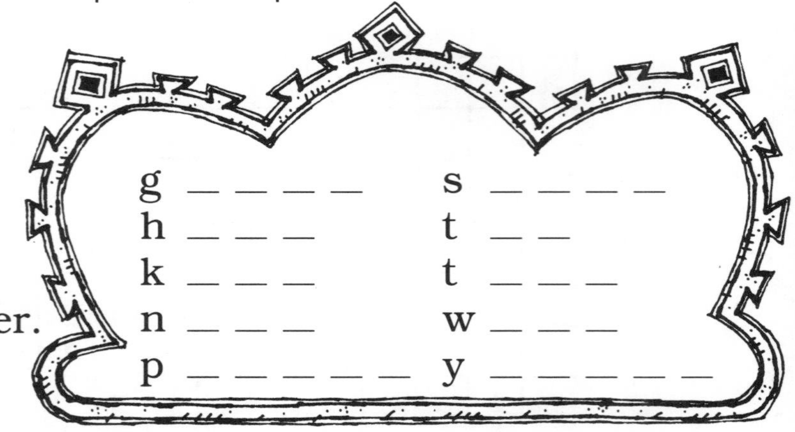

6. **It Doesn't Belong**

Write the one word in each group that does **not** belong with the other three.

(a) black, done, green, yellow

(b) step, most, jump, walk

(c) fast, wet, mud, black

(d) keep, too, green, work

(e) tag, green, truck, today

(f) crown, gold, train, king

(g) soft, park, dark, car

(h) away, baby, today, way

Wordworks

1. **Word Connections**

When you say the word **summer**, do you think of **fun**, **swim**, **holidays**, **camp**, and **picnics**? Say each of the words below. Then write down at least three other words it makes you think of.

(a) rain (b) fast (c) family (d) king (e) mud

2. **Most of All**

Read Marco's story about the park:

I like the park because of the tall slide, the see-saw, and the swings. It's fun to climb the big tree to get into the treehouse. But what I like most about the park are the friends I meet there.

Write a story to tell what you like most about **one** of these:

- the dark
- your family
- mud
- sand
- trains

Did you write what you wanted to say? Read your story to see if you want to make any changes.

Revising and Editing Guide

1. Revising

A.—For Writers

Here are some things to think about when you are looking back at something you have written. You may want to **revise** (make your story or poem better).

1. Did I write what I wanted to say?
2. What was the purpose of this piece of writing?
3. How well does it meet that purpose?
4. Will this writing be interesting for someone else to read?
5. Who might enjoy reading it?
6. How does my piece of writing make me feel?

B.—For Readers

Here are some things to look for when you are reading a classmate's writing and suggesting ways to make it better.

1. Can I guess why my friend wrote this piece?
2. Did my friend meet that purpose?
3. Is there any part of the story I would like to know more about?
4. Did the beginning make me want to read more?
5. Was the story interesting all the way to the end?
6. Is there any part I did not understand?
7. How did this writing make me feel as I read it?

2. Editing

Here are some things to look for when you are checking a classmate's work, or when you are checking your own work.

1. Are all the things that happen written in order?
2. Could more **action words** (like **run**, **say**) and **describing words** (like **blue**, **happy**) be used to make the writing more interesting?
3. Could some short sentences be joined by using words such as **and**, **but**, **or**, **when**, and **because**?
4. Does the piece of writing need a title?
5. Are all of the words spelled correctly? Use a dictionary to check any words that you think may be spelled incorrectly.
6. Does each sentence start with a capital letter?
7. **Proper names** (of persons and places, such as **Lee**, **Canada**) should start with capital letters. Does each proper name start with a capital?
8. Sentences that tell something end with **periods**. Does each telling sentence end with a period?
9. Sentences that ask something end with **question marks** (**?**). Does each question end with a question mark?
10. Are **commas** (**,**) and **quotation marks** (**" "**) used correctly?
11. Each new paragraph should be **indented** (begin a few spaces from the left-hand margin). Is each paragraph indented?
12. Is the printing clear and easy to read?

Superconnections

1. That's Good!

The girl in this picture is doing something **good**. What is she doing?

She is **sharing** her sandwich.
Sharing is a good thing to do.

(a) What **good** things are these people doing? Write a sentence in your notebook for each picture. Tell what good thing each person is doing.

(1)

(2)

(3)

(b) What are some **good** things you like? Write the headings. For each, make a list of good things.

- Good Stories
- Good Foods
- Good Toys
- Good Games
- Good Holidays

2. Leaping Letters

Play leapfrog with letters! Begin at the first letter and leap over every **second** letter to make a word. Like this:

feusn = fun

formobg = frog

(a) Leapfrog these letters. Write the words you make in your notebook.

(1) hmosp
(2) ltobg
(3) heanvoe
(4) srubn
(5) bausloltfarmoeg
(6) jeutmap
(7) roancle
(8) pelpaby

(b) Make up **six** of your own leaping-letter puzzles. See if a friend can leap your letters to find the hiding words.

3. Number Stories

You can use arithmetic to write **number stories**. Like this:

1 + 2 = 3	**One** red brick house + **two** huffs and puffs = **three** safe little pigs.
2–1 = 1	**Two** huffs and puffs – **one** straw house = **one** haystack.

Write three number stories. You may wish to write about the **Three Little Pigs** or storybook characters you like. These arithmetic statements will help you:

3–2 = 1	1 + 2 = 3	1 + 1 = 2	1 + 1 + 1 = 3
2 + 1 = 3	3–1 = 2	2–1 = 1	

4. Falling Leaves

You can put word parts together to make words. Put together the word parts on the falling leaves. How many words can you make? You may use the word parts more than once.

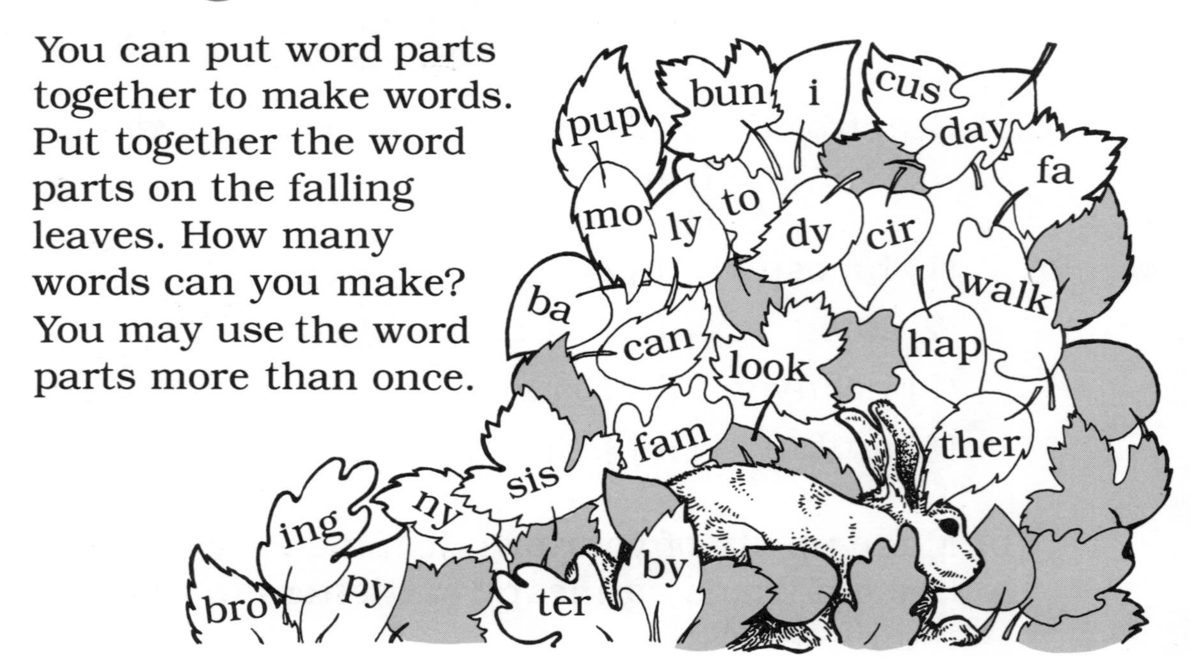

Superconnections

5. Country and City

In the country you might see farms, sheep, and open fields. **In the city** you might see tall buildings, pigeons, and parks.

(a) Copy the chart. Use your own ideas to finish it.

In the country	In the city
You can see...	You can see...
You can hear...	You can hear...
You can eat...	You can eat...
You can go to...	You can go to...
You can play...	You can play...

(b) How are the city and the country the same? How are they different? Write sentences to tell how. Use information from your chart.

6. Changing Words

Can **rats** change into a **star**? They can if you move the letters around. Like this:

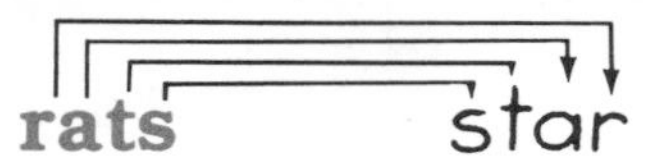

(a) What new word can each of the words below change into? Write the new words. The clues will help you.

(1) Change **are** into a part of your head.

(2) Change **but** into what you take a bath in.

(3) Change **post** into what you cook with.

(4) Change **step** into "cats and dogs."

(b) What can these words change into? Move the letters around until you make new words.

(1) calm	(3) meat	(5) sword	(7) tog
(2) sore	(4) name	(6) tea	(8) mug

7. A Scary Crossword!

Help the ghost finish his crossword puzzle for Hallowe'en. He's written in some letters. Copy the puzzle. Use the **Across** and **Down** clues to help you finish it.

Across

3 A ghost can be _____!

4 Children go out on Hallowe'en _____.

7 "Trick or _____!"

Down

1 You carve this for Hallowe'en.

2 A witch may ride this.

3 Some Hallowe'en costumes can look _____!

5 He's trying to finish this puzzle.

6 A _____ cat is a witch's friend.

8. Animal Rhyme Time

A **hink-pink** is a riddle with two rhyming words for an answer. Like this:

What do you call a street for a frog's cousin?
a toad road

Copy and complete these animal hink-pinks. The words in your answers must rhyme. The picture clues will help you.

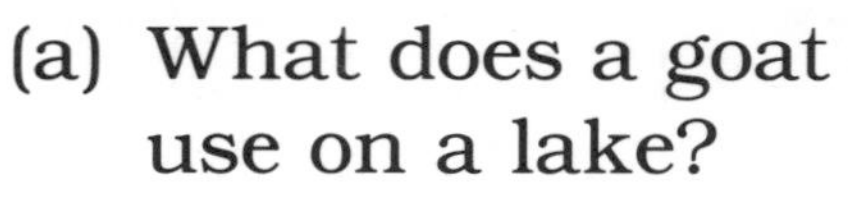

(a) What does a goat use on a lake?
a _ _ _ _
_ _ _ _

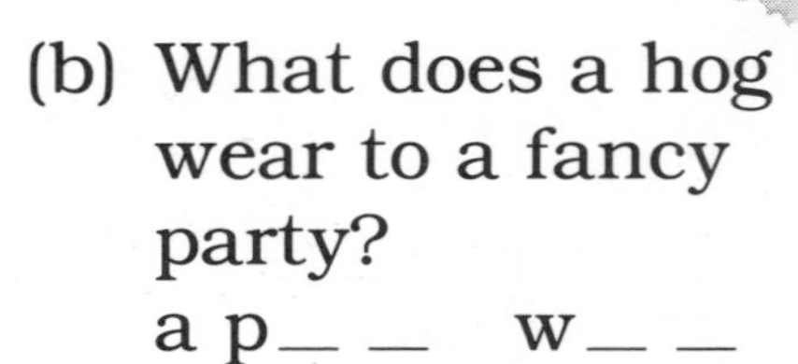

(b) What does a hog wear to a fancy party?
a p_ _ w_ _

(c) Where did the Three Blind Mice live?
in a m_ _ _ _
_ _ _ _ _ _

(d) What is another name for a racetrack?
a h_ _ _ _
c_ _ _ _ _ _

(e) What does a rattlesnake have on her birthday?
a s_ _ _ _
_ _ _ _

(f) What do you call a baby chicken who's not feeling well?
a _ _ _ _
c_ _ _ _

9. Checkerboard Patterns

Play checkerboard! Use each spelling pattern to write one or more new words. For each word you make, you score **one point**.

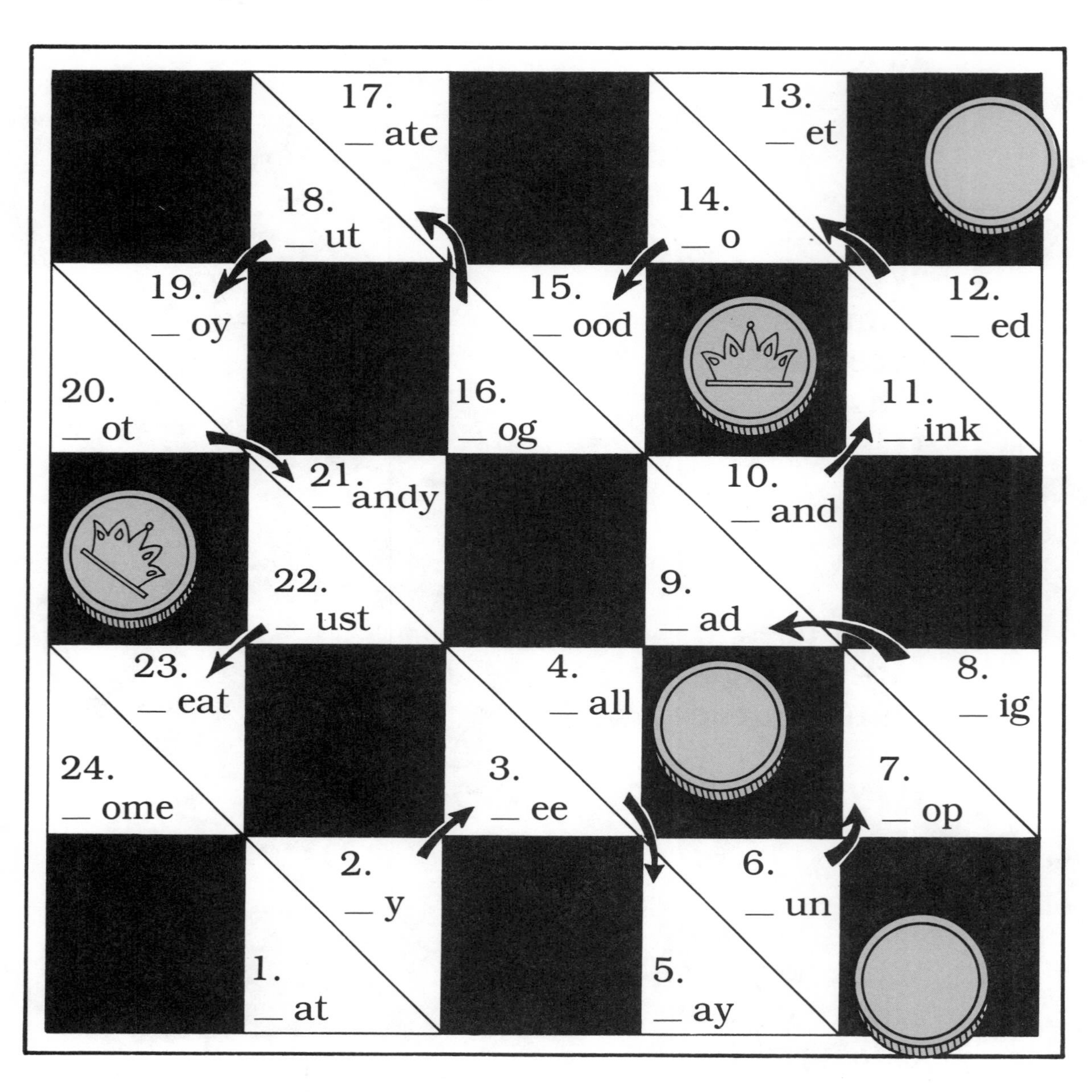

10. Healthy Words

(a) The words on the left are tired. They have been used too many times! Choose a fresh, **healthy word** from the group at the right to use instead of the tired word. For example, a healthy word for **nice** is **wonderful**.

Tired Words

(1) big
(2) said
(3) ran
(4) good
(5) fell
(6) bad
(7) mad
(8) scary

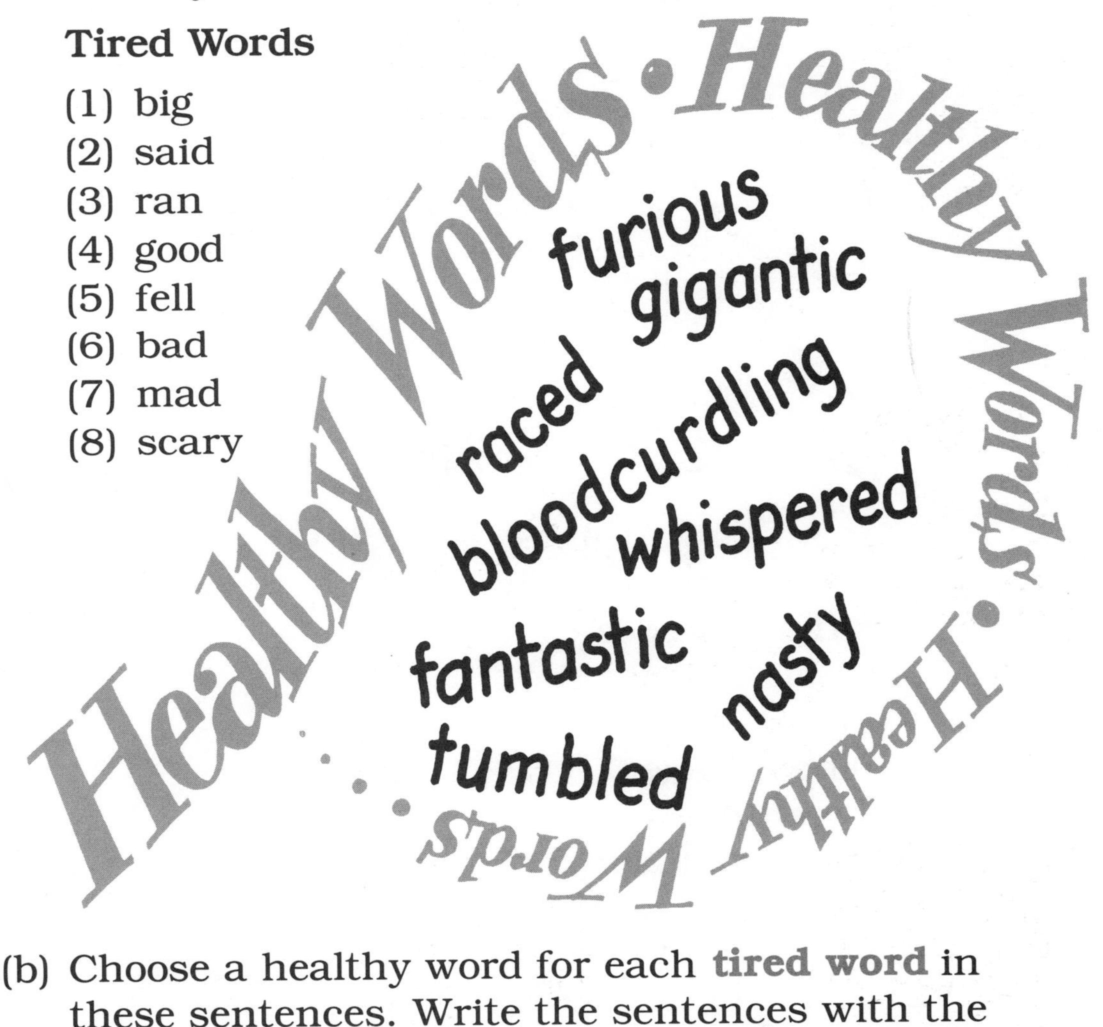

(b) Choose a healthy word for each **tired word** in these sentences. Write the sentences with the new words in your notebook.

(1) Mr. Martin **made** the apple pie.

(2) A **big** truck **went** by us.

(3) The little boy **ate** his soup quickly.

11. What Am I Saying?

This boy is "saying" something **without using words**. What is he saying?

He is saying "**Hello**." We can "say" things with our hands and our bodies.

(a) What are these people "saying"? Write the words.

(1)

(2)

(3)

(b) We can "say" things with our faces. What are these people "saying"? Write the words in your notebook. Then use your own ideas to complete the sentence starters.

(1) I'm _____ because...

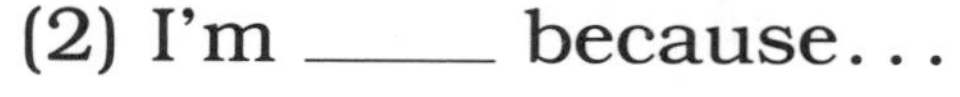

(2) I'm _____ because...

(3) I'm _____ because...

12. Mixed-up Stories

(a) Ms. Welter's computer mixed up the titles to some famous stories. Can you fix them? Read the titles on the printout. Write the correct titles in your notebook.

Red Riding Hood and the Three Bears
Goldilocks and the Seven Dwarfs
Jack and the Big Bad Wolf
The Emperor and the Beanstalk
Snow White and the Grapes
The Fox and His Clothes

(b) Choose one of the **mixed-up** titles from Question (a). Write or tell a story that could have that title.

13. Winter Poems

Here is how you write a special kind of **describing poem**:

First Line: Write a naming word.

Second Line: Write one word describing the naming word.

Third Line: Write two words describing the naming word.

Fourth Line: Write one word describing the naming word.

Fifth Line: Repeat the naming word.

Here is a **winter** describing poem:

winter
cold,
snowy, white,
icy
winter

(a) Use describing words to complete these winter poems:

(1)	(2)	(3)
snowballs	blizzard	toboggan
round,	_____ ,	_____ ,
_____ , _____ ,	_____ , freezing,	_____ , _____ ,
slushy	blizzard	toboggan
snowballs		

(b) Write your own winter describing poem. You may want to draw a picture to go with your poem.

14. What's Wrong?

There are at least **ten** things wrong in this picture. Look carefully. List ten things in your notebook.

15. Where Do You Live?

There are many kinds of **homes**. Choose and write the **home word** that solves each riddle.

Homes			
igloo	apartment	nest	houseboat
tent	trailer	cave	townhouse

(a) I float on the water, but people won't get wet in me. What kind of home am I?

(b) I'm round and cold, but I'm very warm inside. What kind of house am I?

(c) Families fly away from me. I'm made of twigs and leaves. What kind of home am I?

(d) Bears like me, especially in the winter when they sleep. What kind of home am I?

(e) I like to travel with people. They pull me on my wheels. What kind of home am I?

(f) I'm usually in a row of houses. What kind of house am I?

(g) Many of me are together in one building. What kind of home am I?

(h) You can fold me up and take me with you. What kind of home am I?

16. Take a Word Trip!

Max took a **word trip**. He wrote the word **story**. Next he wrote a word that **story** made him think of (**book**). Then he wrote what **book** made him think of (**read**). He kept going until his word trip ended at **leave**.

(a) Make your own word trips. Start with each word below and keep going until you have at least six new words. See how long you can make each word trip.

(1) orange (2) game (3) mom (4) fly

(b) Choose **one** of your word trips. Write a story that it makes you think of.

17. Words in Valentines

Mitsu picked out different letters from this word and juggled them around:

about

Here are the new words she made:

a to out bat boa boat tub tab at but

(a) See how many words you can write using the letters in **valentines**. You may use each letter only once in a new word. If you can make at least **ten** words, you are a real Word Wizard!

(b) Choose your own big word. Give it to a friend. How many small words can your friend make with the letters in your word?

18. In the Cookie Jar

(a) There are ten **number words** hiding in this cookie jar. The words go down and across. Write the words in your notebook. If you find all **ten**, you are an expert Number Muncher! The first word is **six**.

(b) Here is a poem that uses **number words**:

Two hungry puppies,
One kind young girl,
Eight shiny bones,
Two puppies jumping for joy!

Write your own number-word poem. Use some of the words you found in the cookie jar.

19. Scrambled Food Words

(a) Be a word cook! Unscramble the food words on the shelves. Write the new words in your notebook.

(b) Now you're cooking! Write the words you made in Part (a) in **a b c** order.

20. Elemenno/LMNO

Play **Elemenno**! Pick some letters in a row from the alphabet. Choose words that start with those letters. Make silly sentences with the words. Like this:

B icycles
C an
D rive
E very
F riday.

(a) Finish these Elemennos. Use interesting words.

(1) Quick
Robots
Say
T

(2) Giants
Have
Interesting
Jumping
K

(3) Dogs
Everywhere
Forget
G
H

(b) Make up your own Elemenno. Draw a picture of your sentence if you want. These words may help you:

boy	see	can
ran	don't	eat
play	animals	

21. Missing Questions!

Here is an answer: **a red ball**. What **questions** could you ask to give that answer?

- What did I lose today? *a red ball*
- What shall we play with? *a red ball*
- What does my dog love to chase? *a red ball*

(a) Here are some answers. Write **three questions** for each answer.

(1) a peanut-butter sandwich

(2) my top two front teeth

(3) on the train at three o'clock

(4) to get to school on time

(b) On the left are some more answers. Write **questions** that might be asked by the people on the right.

Answers	Question asked by:
(1) a tasty birthday cake	a baker a customer
(2) to get a kitten down from a tree	a child a firefighter
(3) downtown	a friend a taxi driver

22. Under the Big Top

Can you find the fourteen **circus words** hidden under the big top? The words go down and across. Write the words in your notebook. If you find all **fourteen**, you are a Super Circus Performer! The first word is **trapeze**.

y	b	c	e	h	t	r	a	p	e	z	e
z	x	d	g	c	h	i	l	d	r	e	n
a	f	w	u	f	u	n	o	z	k	n	a
p	b	r	v	t	i	g	e	r	r	n	m
n	q	c	u	s	r	m	q	l	d	s	r
m	e	l	e	p	h	a	n	t	z	w	x
l	v	o	b	t	g	s	f	e	b	c	t
k	z	w	q	z	n	t	h	n	e	l	b
p	o	n	y	w	a	e	d	t	f	b	k
a	j	k	l	m	k	r	c	u	n	c	n
r	i	c	r	b	d	o	d	q	a	w	z
a	h	i	g	f	s	m	l	u	v	p	x
d	a	r	e	d	e	v	i	l	t	x	u
e	k	c	d	c	a	i	o	p	s	g	n
n	l	u	g	h	l	j	n	b	l	b	o
p	m	s	b	a	z	d	x	t	e	q	s

23. Good Rules

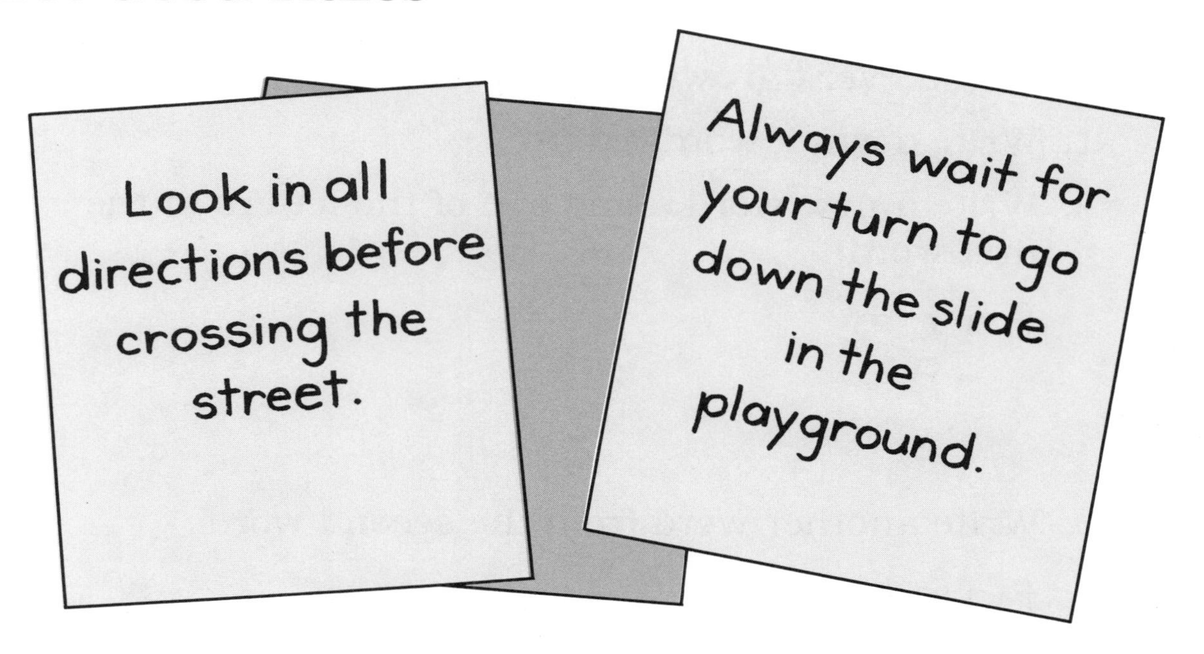

When we work and play at home, outdoors, and in school we need **rules**. Rules about safety and politeness help make sure that everyone has fun and no one gets hurt.

(a) Write your own list of **ten** Good Rules. These sentence starters may help you:

- You should always. . .when you. . .
- Make sure you. . .because. . .
- When you. . .be sure to. . .so that. . .

(b) You and a partner may wish to make a book called **Good Rules**. Choose **ten** safety and politeness rules. Check the spelling and punctuation. Draw pictures for some of your rules. Your teacher will help you put your book together. Share your **Good Rules** book with friends and people in your family.

Superconnections

24. Growing Words

Have you ever "**grown**" words? Here's how you do it:

1. Write down a word: farm
2. Write a new word using one of the letters in the first word:

```
f a r m
    a
    k
    e
```

3. Write another word from the second word:

```
f a r m
    a
    kitchen
    e
```

4. Keep going! Write as many words as you can.

(a) **Grow** these words. The first one is started for you. Add at least **five** more words to each one.

(1) tractor (2) pony (3) corn

```
tractor
 u
 n
 t
```

(b) Here's another way to **grow** words:

(1) Start with a single letter: d

(2) Add one letter to make a word: do

(3) Add one more letter to make another word: dog

(4) Make more words by adding one letter at a time.

Grow at least **three** words from each of these letters.

n t b

25. Mixed-up House

(a) Help the movers! Unscramble these words that name things found in a **house**. Move them into the house in alphabetical order.

tthbaub	malp
evtos	tveeliiosn
sedshi	ariod
awhser	racept
rdyre	ebd

(b) The items on the left below were put into the wrong rooms. Write each group of items in your notebook. Beside each group, write the room where the items belong.

Items	Room They Were Put Into
(1) soap, towel, washcloth	kitchen
(2) sheets, blankets, pillow	toolshed
(3) spoons, plates, pots	bathroom
(4) lawnmower, rake, shovel	bedroom

26. A Royal Message

(a) King William has written a secret message. Can you decode it? He left out all of the **vowels**: **a**, **e**, **i**, **o**, **u**. Rewrite his message in your notebook. Put the vowels in the right places to read his secret message.

D_ _r Fr_ _nd,
Th_s m_ss_g_ _s v_ry
_mp_rt_nt. Y_ _ m_st try t_ b_
_t th_ c_stl_ _n Fr_d_y n_ght _t
_ _ght _'cl_ck. Th_ Q_ _ _n w_ll
_nt_r th_ h_ll _t th_t t_m_. W_
w_ll _ll j_mp _ _t _nd y_ll
"H_ppy B_rthd_y!" C_n y_ _ c_m_?
Pl_ _s_ r_ply.
Th_nk y_ _.
Y_ _r K_ng

(b) Write your reply to King William using his secret code. See if a friend can decode your message.

27. A Moving Crossword

Copy and complete this crossword about things that **move**. The **Across** and **Down** clues will help you.

Across

2 This moves using a sail.

6 This moves on two wheels.

7 This moves by paddling.

8 This moves on tracks.

11 You move on ice with these.

Down

1 This moves in the water.

3 This moves high up without wings.

4 This moves down snowy hills.

5 This moves in space.

7 This moves on streets and highways.

8 This carries many things in it when it moves.

9 This moves very fast up in the sky.

10 This carries many people when it moves.

28. A Code in the Mud

(a) Sue wrote a message in the mud. She used this secret code. Break the code by matching each number with its letter partner. Write Sue's message in your notebook.

a	b	c	d	e	f	g	h	i	j	k	l	m
1	2	3	4	5	6	7	8	9	10	11	12	13

n	o	p	q	r	s	t	u	v	w	x	y	z
14	15	16	17	18	19	20	21	22	23	24	25	26

8•9!/ 13•25/ 14•1•13•5/ 9•19/ 19•21•5./ 4•15/
25•15•21/ 12•9•11•5/ 20•15/ 23•1•12•11/ 9•14/
13•21•4?/ 9•20/ 9•19/ 19•15•6•20/ 1•14•4/
23•5•20/ 1•14•4/ 2•12•1•3•11./ 9/ 12•9•11•5/
20•15/ 16•12•1•25/ 9•14/ 13•21•4./ 3•1•14/
25•15•21/ 13•1•11•5/ 1/ 13•21•4/ 16•9•5?/
20•5•12•12/ 13•5/ 8•15•23./

(b) Tell Sue how to make a **mud pie**. Write the steps. These sentence starters may help you:

- You will need...
- First you...
- Next you...
- Use some...to...
- Then you...
- When you are done...

29. Letters in the Sand

It's fun to write in wet sand. Like this:

Write at least **five** messages you would like to write in the sand. See how many of these words you can use.

need	work	sand	(**your name**)
dog	took	today	let
print	away	party	me

30. An A B C of School Fun

What happened in your school this year? Try to use each letter of the alphabet to start a word or group of words. Each word in your list should tell about something that happened in school. The words might be names of things you talked or read about in class. They might be games you played or the names of some of your friends.

Here is how Mitsu started her list:

A rithmetic
B irthday party
C arlo's story
D ancing
E

Word List

Word List